Father Knows

ZILCH

Father Knows

ZILCH

A GUIDE FOR
DUMBFOUNDED DADS

LINWOOD BARCLAY

Stoddart

Published in 1996 by
Stoddart Publishing Co. Limited
34 Lesmill Road
Toronto, Canada
M3B 2T6
Tel. (416) 445-3333
Fax (416) 445-5967

Stoddart Books are available for bulk purchase for sales promotions,
premiums, fundraising, and seminars. For details, contact the **Special Sales
Department** at the above address.

Canadian Cataloguing in Publication Data

Barclay, Linwood
Father knows zilch : a guide for dumbfounded dads

ISBN 0-7737-5808-9

1. Fatherhood — Humor. 2. Fathers — Humor.
I. Title.

PS8553.A73F3 1996   C818'.5402   C95-933269-3
PR9199.3.B37F3 1996

Cover Design: the boy 100 and Tannice Goddard
Computer Graphics: Mary Bowness
Illustrations: Steve Nease

Printed and bound in Canada

*Stoddart Publishing gratefully acknowledges the support of the Canada
Council, and the Ontario Arts Council, in the development of writing and
publishing in Canada.*

For Neetha,
Spencer, and Paige;
loving family, meal ticket

Contents

Introduction

(Or: Why, with all the fatherhood books out there, this is the one you absolutely, positively, without a shadow of a doubt do not need, but must have)

Okay, dads, when's the last time you sat down and read a book or a magazine or a newspaper article offering advice on how to become a better father? Something that went even further than mere practical tips, but got right into the nitty-gritty about what it really MEANS to be a father?

Hello?

The fact is, fathers love their children very much, and they want to be the best fathers in the whole entire world, but, unlike mothers, they don't want to have to READ about how to get that way. They feel no need to get a grasp of the big picture.

Suppose they open a fatherhood book and read something like: "Paleontologists believe it was Cro-Magnon man who first got in touch with his paternal feelings, who first strove to articulate his sense of wonder that life could spring forth from his loins."

Most dads will look up from the page and say: "Where's the sports section?" Or possibly: "What are loins?"

They figure that all they'll ever need to know about raising kids will come to them naturally, through experience, the same way it did with their own fathers.

But women, as we've said, are far more inclined to read about issues surrounding parenting.

This is no surprise, since from the moment they become pregnant, their bodies are thrown into a tailspin. Who WOULDN'T go looking for more information when your breasts are swelling, you're ralphing before dawn, and rapidly losing sight of your feet?

If men went through ANYTHING physiological in the creation of their children, there would be entire government ministries devoted to dispensing information to put them at ease. There would be a New York Fatherhood Exchange. Every fall, there would be a Dad Bowl.

But seeing how a man's contribution to the reproductive cycle can be measured in the time it takes to air a beer commercial, it's little wonder that they'd rather read about fuel injection or point spreads.

In fact, most things fathers read have no real practical value whatsoever.

They read about sports they are too old to play, about cars they are not wealthy enough to own, about travel destinations they cannot find time to visit.

That is why this is THE guide for those kinds of fathers. Not only will it keep them occupied long enough to stay out of everyone else's hair, demanding to know who put that empty milk carton back in the fridge or who tried to jam a pizza carton into an already overflowing garbage receptacle under the kitchen sink, BUT ALSO, the information contained in these pages will not tax them.

It will not challenge them.

It will not make them think.

In fact, we'll bet you there's not a dad out there who'll be able to read this book and come away with even one, practical, realistic bit of advice.

If there is, this book will be a complete failure.

Father Knows
ZILCH

1

Are You Dad Material?

(Or: "Can I be a caring, loving, attentive father without having to touch anything especially icky?")

A lot of questions run through the minds of men who are on the verge of fatherhood. They include:

Am I up to it?

Can I give a child the love he needs?

Will I have to curtail my championship belching, so as to provide a good example? (Unless it's a boy, in which case will my belching be good *enough*?)

How will having a child change my relationship with my wife? Is this a good time to tell her I actually had a vasectomy five years ago?

The fact is, no potential dad ever knows the answers to these questions until after he's been through those months leading up to the birth of his child, been with his wife at that moment when his child hits the atmosphere, and held that beautiful newborn in his arms, all the while thinking that this is it, this has defined his purpose in life, this has brought everything into focus.

In other words: "I'm going to have to trade in the Miata convertible for a minivan."

How Do You Know If You're Ready?

Based on exhaustive surveys (five, six phone calls, easy) of fathers-to-be, we've come up with several of the most compelling reasons men come up with for having children. Where do you fit in? Take a look at the following and see.

1. Making them is fun, unless you throw your back out or pull a hamstring at an inopportune moment.
2. Your wife's *told* you you're obviously ready, because when your friends the Glebemonts had *their* little girl, you couldn't take your eyes off her.

   (Your memory of this is a little different. You seem to recall that you couldn't stop looking at her because, at three weeks, she looked just like the Wicked Witch of the West from *The Wizard of Oz*, only her nose was not quite as cute.)
3. You don't want to leave this world without making your mark.

   What could be better than bringing into this world a namesake? As you get into your 20s and 30s, this idea becomes especially appealing, because it's obvious this may be the *only* way that mark will ever be made.

   After all, the initial time commitment to fathering a child is only a couple of minutes, as opposed to building a career, which can often involve 12- to 14-hour days and lots of boring meetings, unless you are fortunate enough to get a job with your daddy's company, and can spend your time perfecting your paper-airplane-building skills.
4. You're dying to revive your interest in model trains, Dinky Toys, baseball cards, comic books, all Warner Brothers cartoons, Nintendo games, and the Thunderbirds puppet/adventure show, but you need a cover story.

Over the years, wives have become quite used to the male obsession with sports, even if they are less than crazy about how much time it eats up. But the average wife is unprepared for the fact that her husband, given a choice between seeing her model a new Warner's push-up number or playing with his son's new radio-controlled dune buggy, will still be standing in the driveway trying to master leaping the curb without flipping the buggy over long after she's fallen asleep for the night. (Free tip: To avoid suspicion, do not buy that $5,000 remote-control helicopter until the child is at least two months old.)

5. You're Prince Charles, and need some heirs to the throne.

6. You're an appliance repairman named Goobenson and when Floyd, the sign painter, did your truck he spelled it "Goob and Son." Rather than hurt Floyd's feelings, you have your name shortened and decide it's time to have a kid.

7. You're allergic to dogs, and whenever you get a goldfish, it dies. You think you might have better luck with a kid, since they respond better to errors in overfeeding.

8. You might as well have a child, because now that all the big movies are *Batman*, *Die Hard*, and *Lethal Weapon* sequels or rehashes of old TV shows like *Mission: Impossible* or *The Addams Family*, it's not worth going to the show anymore.

9. You've had a lifelong interest in drool, having done graduate work in this area, and since you're neither young enough nor old enough now to produce your own in large enough quantities, a baby seems just the ticket.

10. Your parents, in-laws, and buddies are all convinced you haven't got what it takes to be a dad, that maybe you're shooting BLANKS (*heh-heh*), so you must prove them wrong.

    This assumes, of course, that being able to father a child has something to do with manliness, which it does not. It has more to do with being in the right place at the right time.

11. You feel left out when your other friends, the ones who

already have children, discuss bowel movements all through dinner when they have you over.

12. You've gotten somebody pregnant. This is undeniable proof that, at least physiologically, you have what it takes to be a dad.

If you're lucky, this pregnant person is somebody you know. It might even be somebody you'd like to spend the rest of your life with. If you're really lucky, that person will be your wife. If you're already married, and this person you've gotten pregnant is not your wife, you might want to check out my other book of advice, *Keeping Your Pants On: A Good Plan*.

So how did you do? If you answered "Yes" to one or more of the preceding questions, you're probably ready for one of life's greatest adventures.

But you should be aware that if you're going to become a father, there are certain risks. Chief among them is the condition we'll describe in the following section.

Testicular Destruction

One way to spot a father, particularly a father of children aged three and over, is his extreme sensitivity to potential damage to his nether regions.

Even men who have spent their youth engaged in such gruelling, painful activities as football, rugby, hockey, and cycling (YIKES, *especially* cycling), where being injured in the gonadal region is not an uncommon occurrence, are completely unprepared for what awaits them as fathers.

Just as a young child's finger is drawn instinctively to explore the inner workings of his nose, so, too, are other parts of his body inherently designed to inflict damage upon the father.

This starts at an early age, usually once the child is able to walk briskly. Here is a typical scene:

Proud Papa, sitting on his haunches, elbows resting on knees, is encouraging his young daughter to walk across the room.

"That's it! Yes, that's it, my little princess!" His arms are outstretched. His daughter, teetering on her obnoxiously cute Weebok running shoes, takes another unsteady step toward him.

When she is but one foot away, she pitches forward, missing her father's arms, and turns her head into a rapidly moving projectile that resembles a torpedo from the U.S.S. *Polaris*.

"Come on, honey, you can do it, yes you *AWWWWWWWWWW* . . . *GODDD!*"

This is only the beginning. Just wait until a child can run.

Daddy: Hey, everybody, Daddy's home!

Child: (running from the kitchen) Daddy! Daddy! Daddy! I really missed you!

Daddy: I missed you too, sweetheart. Come here and give Daddy a hug!

Child: (still running, a little faster now, arms out for a hug, getting ready to move head into position) Did you bring me anything? Did you get me *(head now moving a notch lower, getting ready)* anything? Is there anything for me in *(only a millisecond away now, torpedo loaded, just waiting for the command . . .)* the car or —

Daddy: Now, you know I can't bring you something EVERY day, sweet —

Child: — in your briefcase *(head snaps down into position and . . . FIRE!)*

Daddy: — heart *OHHHHMYYYYGOOOODDDDD!!!!!!!* Honey! Oh God, honey, get me an icepack!

This is all part of an elaborate, instinctive defense mechanism that can be found in all children. Even though the child is unaware of her motivations, she's doing everything she can at the earliest stages to make sure she's the ONLY child in the household. (For more information on this, see Chapter 5, "Sex.")

If the child can prevent further siblings from coming into the family, she'll always be the center of everything, always have her parents' undivided attention, and never have to share her Barbies or favorite blanky. Every child instinctively aims to be a Spoiled Brat.

This phenomenon exists even in large families. No matter how many kids there are, it's always the fear of the youngest that there might be one more. And then his or her status as the treasured, pampered, spoiled baby of the family would be lost forever. It's definitely preferable to share your parents with just five other brothers and sisters, than six.

There's no better way to accomplish this than taking dead aim at the equipment that gets the whole ball rolling, as it were. It's just like in any war: you take out the opponent's weapon sites first.

Walking and running children are not the only kinds you must be on guard for. This kind of attack can be launched at any time, when you least expect it. Such attacks are frequently launched from the seemingly safe environment of the family room couch, in front of the television.

You're snuggled up next to your son, watching the movie *Home Alone* (basically TWO HOURS of guys getting pounded in the testicular area by a youngster, which accounts for the huge popularity of this flick among children), when you get to that part where Kevin says triumphantly: "Yesss!"

Kids like to say this along with him, making two fists and swinging them downward suddenly. One of these fists will always find its way into your lap. If by some chance the child's grandfather is sitting on the other side, he can nail two at once.

This is why it has now become customary for the buddies of a new father, once he's finished passing out the cigars, to pitch in and buy him a jockstrap made out of titanium steel.

Just remember that this is mostly for wearing around the house, and *not* on the golf course, where it is guaranteed to attract lightning when a storm approaches. (YOU DO NOT WANT THIS TO HAPPEN TO YOU.)

Jealousy

If they're completely honest with themselves, many fathers-to-be will admit that the thing they're most worried about is sharing their wives' attention with the new little one.

"The baby, the baby," they hear some other new fathers say. "Everything's THE BABY. There's never any time for ME."

Many men will actually start *acting* like a baby in order to get their wives' attention. This most often takes the form of perpetual whining, complaining constantly that they are not being fed enough, and trying to nurse at completely inconvenient times.

It doesn't have to be this way. All you have to do is have as strong an interest in the new baby as your wife does. Share in the feedings (once the child is on a *bottle*, of course, unless you are the Amazing Bearded Lady), do more than your share of the diaper changes, throw in a load of laundry without being asked.

Sharing fully in the experience will not only deepen the bond you already have with your mate, but it'll bring about that wondrous thing that fathers treasure deeply their whole lives: nooky rights.

Other Requirements

Finally, there are a few other characteristics you should have before embarking on fatherhood, many of which we will explore in depth throughout this book — unless we get distracted by a *Twilight Zone* marathon on cable.

You must be able to discipline, but still be nurturing, as in: "WHAT THE HELL DID YOU THINK YOU WERE DOING, PUTTING ON TAP SHOES AND DOING A BROADWAY NUMBER ON THE HOOD OF MY CAR!!!!! My precious little angel."

You must be patient. For example, even though children's neverending questions can be exasperating, you must do your best to provide detailed responses to such seemingly trivial queries as:

"Why is that car blue?"

"Why is it raining?"

"Why is that a cat?"

"Why was Mom kissing the furnace repairman while you were upstairs playing computer pinball?"

And lastly, know that there's no perfect way to raise children.

You're not going to be right all the time.

You're going to make mistakes, just as your own parents did.

But times have changed. As we approach the end of this century, you can take comfort in the knowledge that when your own kids grow up, if you did make any mistakes, they'll hire Johnnie Cochran and come back and sue your ass off.

2

The Early Years

(Or: "Don't worry, it gets better — HA HA, gotcha")

Although this book is intended primarily to help fathers deal with the kinds of situations that can develop with young children, as opposed to infants, it seems only right that we spend a chapter going over some of the things you'll need to know about taking care of babies and toddlers.

Many of the attitudes you form and adjustments you learn to make during your child's earliest years will serve you well for as long as you have kids living under your roof.

These are formative years — not just for the new child, but for the new father as well. While the child learns to recognize the world around him, to know the voice of his parents, to yearn for the touch of a human hand, the father, now a model of responsibility, is busy trying to trade in his hang glider for a nursery intercom system.

Social scientists have studied the changes in the new father and have discovered that he goes through several observable changes. Here's what they've found:

The father's stages of development

First month	Second month	Third month
• newfound interest in things domestic, like doing the wash, cooking.	• tentatively asks spouse if she's feeling, you know, just the teensiest bit romantic.	• always offering to do the shopping, especially when baby cries a lot, and mall is in another county.
• singing nursery rhymes.	• reprints all of Stephen King's *The Stand* (the revised, LONGER version) on the side of the local Lions club.	• now that baby is on bottle for night feedings, keeps asking wife if this is really in child's best interest — a baby really needs his mother at 3 a.m.
• buying lots of toys, like 1/24-scale race car kits, which he's busy assembling to decorate child's room.	• tries to engage baseball-mad co-workers in interesting stories about cloth vs. disposable diapers.	
• shows sympathy by saying: "Gee, if you weren't nursing, I'd be happy to get up at night and feed the baby. But since you are, could you not turn on the light when you get up?"	• shoots 73 rolls of film of new baby and sells high chair to pay for the processing.	• late for work twice in one week after sleeping through alarm; boss says sleeping on the job not good when you're an air traffic controller.
• feeling horny, but doesn't want to put pressure on anyone, so buys a wood-burning kit; within a week, has reprinted all of Moby Dick onto 12 sheets of plywood.	• finally figures out how to get baby's foot into sock.	• keeps confusing Pablum powder with Parmesan; ruins Caesar salad when the in-laws come over for dinner.
	• changes first diaper without saying: "Thar she blows!"	
	• leaves home with spit-up in hair.	

A Change in Sensibilities and Interests

Your sensibilities begin to change even before your child is born — sometimes right in the operating room, in the moments preceding your child's debut.

Parts of your wife's body that you'd previously only considered in a more romantic context (as an integral part of your personal entertainment system, in fact) are being poked and prodded and examined and hooked up to monitors by total strangers dressed in surgical gowns and white gloves. It doesn't make the moment seem any more intimate to know that these are trained, medical professionals who are wondering if they'll still make their tee-off time.

Suddenly this woman you've loved, worshiped, and — most of all — respected since the moment you first spent time with her in the back of your parents' Pacer has lost all her privacy, is in intense pain, and is, along with you, facing the most awesome responsibility in the world: a new life. And it can all be traced back to that most intimate of moments between two people.

This kind of realization can, with some men, put them off the idea of sex for some time, often for as long as a week.

Other interests change as well.

If someone had told you back in university, when you pondered metaphysical questions like whether Carlsberg could be chugged more easily than Heineken, that someday you'd find a child's production of waste material engrossing instead of just gross, you'd have felt morally obligated to chug another beer to put the thought out of your head.

But it's true. Married couples spend hours discussing this subject without the slightest thought of retching. The phone lines are burning up with this kind of talk.

"Hello?"

"Sorry to bother you at work, but Junior filled his diaper again and he's just fine!"

"What a trooper!"

11

Not only that, parents spend hours comparing notes with *other* new parents, although this does not, thankfully, usually extend beyond conversation to actual slide displays.

You haven't seen this kind of obsession with the bodily functions of another human being since your own father interrogated you and your brother, trying to determine the source of some foul emanation.

Fortunately, there was always the dog to take the fall.

Expanding Your Base of Knowledge

Becoming a father expands your world exponentially — it's as if an entire new universe has opened up. When you bring a new life into the world, you start imagining what it must be like to see it for the first time.

Words you knew before now have entirely different meanings, as in the sentence: "Are these nipples sterilized?"

And new words come into your vocabulary: diaper rash and diarrhea, placenta and playtime, burps and blankys, formula and foul aromas, strained peas and Slinkys, selflessness and sleeplessness, Handi Wipes and Toys "R" Us, Osh-Kosh and Robert Munsch, Penelope Leach and toys for the beach, Huggies and goodnight hugs, colic and croup, constipation and circumcision, whooping cough and Weeboks, wet pants and training pants, amniocentesis and Uncle Remus, discipline and drool, Fisher-Price and head lice, Barney and bedwetting, maternity benefits and paternity leave, Pampers and Pablum, Gerber and "Gimme dat!" chicken pox and cradle cap, teething and the midnight feeding, and, Fatigue, Fatigue, Fatigue.

Yes, especially Fatigue.

It's not just all the work that a new baby entails. You're exhausted from learning and being exposed to so many different things, including your wife's new nursing bra, a contraption so unlike anything you've ever seen in any Victoria's Secret catalog that it scares you.

Some child experts say first-time mothers and fathers are weary all the time because they never get a decent sleep, what with being up several times in the night to feed a hungry or crying baby. But it's really just a case of information overload.

To cope with this, you must lie down frequently to give your brain a chance to absorb it all. It can also help to watch things on TV that have no informational value whatsoever, like a Stallone movie, or the Parliamentary channel.

You tend, after awhile, to view everything as a learning experience and can become quite excited about the smallest of projects.

For example, one day you find that your wife has purchased a new horn for your child's tricycle, even though your newborn is a long ways away from being able to use one, and you haven't even bought the tricycle yet.

Well, you can sure take care of that. So you race off to the bike shop and choose one. It has a red frame and white spokes. Plastic streamers hang off the handlebar grips. The moment you return home you get out your tools and attach that horn. When your wife gets home you proudly show off your handiwork. There's no question she's impressed. Her mouth drops open and she says: "What the hell have you done with my breast pump?"

Household Hazards

It's especially important when you have an infant that you start thinking about household hazards, because if you don't you could get yourself killed.

Oh sure, you should lock up poisonous chemicals and put away anything small enough for a child to swallow. That goes without saying. But what about you? Isn't your life worth something, too?

The hazards posed to the father of a new child are endless. They include the following.

Back Problems

You might think your little baby doesn't weigh all that much, and that you could hardly throw your back out carrying her around the house, but wait until you go for a short drive to a friend's house to show her off.

First, you must get her safely belted into one of those padded buckets they make for newborns that, while extremely cumbersome, only weigh 153 pounds. Then you have to lug her *and* the contraption out to the car and belt her in once again into the backseat.

So far you've managed to hold onto your two-door Japanese sports car — just because you're now a family doesn't mean you have to get a family *car*. But it does mean that, while trying to maneuver this bucket full of child, you must push ahead the front passenger seat, and have the skills of a contortionist to lift her into the back.

A passing pedestrian will observe you with one foot on the pavement, one on the floor of the backseat, your butt folding the front seat down onto itself (a good tip is to do this when there's no one sitting in that spot), your head scrunched under the roof, sweat pouring down the side of your head and forming puddles in the upholstery.

You're likely to be heard saying something sweet to your child to distract her from all the jostling, something like: "After Daddy gets you in the car, Daddy's going back into the house to see if he can find a heating pad that runs off a car cigarette lighter so that he won't cramp up *completely* by the time we get to wherever it is your mother's decided we should show you off."

But the way back into the house is impeded by a few items your wife says you need to take along for this short visit: a cooler filled with enough made-up bottles to take you through to her first prom; a playpen; a case filled with 35 backup outfits should she start spitting up like Mount Pinatubo; 5 outfits for her mother should the eruption land on her; 3 bags of baby toys; 2 special blankets; the entire Sesame Street collection of stuffed toys; a baby swing; a

stroller; a hopelessly tangled mess of bungee cords and pads and string called a Jolly Jumper; and, finally, the Hoover, since sometimes the sound of a vacuum cleaner is soothing and helps the baby get to sleep.

Now you're REALLY sorry about not trading this two-door Japanese car in on something slightly larger, like an aircraft carrier, because the only thing you can get into the trunk is the cooler.

You pull out of the driveway and are halfway down the block when you ask your wife:

"Where is it, exactly, that we're going this afternoon —"

15

"Oh stop! This is it! Turn in at this driveway!"

You are, it turns out, visiting the couple five doors down, who already have a child of their own and are DYING to see the new addition to your family.

Now you get to go through the whole process in reverse, only this time, because you're visiting a home where there resides another guy, just like you, who also has a child and instinctively *knows* the kind of day you are having, you're expecting him to help you lug some of this stuff inside.

Boy, are you new at this.

As soon as your wife goes in their house with the new baby, this couple will surround the two of them, saying things like: "Oooohhhhh, she's SO beautiful." Actually, the guy will probably say HE'S so beautiful, because men, who have a hard enough time remembering the sex of their own children, can never remember the sex or name of their friends' infants.

But he will be required to stay at his wife's side and go "ooohhhh" and "aaahhhh," lest his wife begins to think he doesn't absolutely love not just his own baby, but every baby in the entire world.

They will all disappear far into the house while you struggle with their screen door, banging the end of the playpen into the glass, dropping the cooler on your foot, and spilling Big Bird out of the toy bag onto the front stoop where he is immediately pounced upon by your friends' cat.

And your back is KILLING YOU.

Tripping
There are now enough expandable child-safety gates in your house to give it the feel of a federal penitentiary. At the bottom of the stairs, at the top of the stairs, at the entrance into the dining room, at the door to the backyard. Gates are everywhere.

These removable gates, seemingly intended to keep your crawling/walking child out of danger, are actually there to make life more exciting for you.

16

It is inevitable that one day you'll fail to see one of these gates and go tumbling over it, and we can say with some certainty that it will be that gate positioned at the TOP of a very long flight of uncarpeted stairs.

Some good can come from this, however. Many fathers report that after taking such a tumble, they witness their children laughing, right out loud, for the very first time.

"Aww, honey," your wife will say, "fall down the stairs for her just one more time. Did you see her face when you did that?"

Talking Funny

When you have a baby, you start to talk funny.

You purse your lips up in a strange way. You make your eyes roll. And then your voice goes deep and you say: "Daddums wuvs his wittel darling, Daddums do."

You find yourself talking like this all the time you are around the baby. It starts to become second nature. You aren't even aware that it's happening. And then, before you know it, you're starting to talk like this at inopportune times.

"Did you know I clocked you back there doing 60 in a 40?"

"Daddums didn't see da sign, Mr. Poweece Ossifer. Daddums make big boo-boo."

"Well, Daddums is going to haul his ass out of the car now and see if he can walk a straight line for the nice policeman."

When They Get a Little Older . . .

Once a child is beyond the toddler stage and can dress herself, roam about the house freely without your worrying that she'll fall down the stairs, get in a car and do up her seatbelt without assistance, turn on the TV, make herself a bowl of cereal, even cross the street safely, you'll find that your life tends to settle down a bit.

You're able to put aside so many of your previous worries, but these will quickly be taken over by a whole set of new ones, like

17

whether she's getting a proper education, learning how to cope with the added responsibilities growing up brings, or dating the president of the local chapter of the Satan's Choice motorcycle gang.

While you may no longer have to get up in the middle of the night to help with feedings, or get up early with an infant who likes to start her day with the roosters, you can rest assured you'll never get a good night's sleep for the rest of your life.

3
Eating Right

(Or: Don't forget the wax fruit)

Just because you're a dad, and just because your idea of fine dining is a chili dog with cheese (whoa, where can we get one of those RIGHT NOW?), there's no reason for anyone to think you don't know a thing or two about ensuring that your child eats right.

And to prove to the rest of the world that you can tell Twinkies from Tempura, take the following skill-testing quiz and wave the results around in their smug, doubting faces.

Known as the "Dads' Official Nutritional Understanding Test" (DONUT), it determines how well you understand that young minds and bodies depend heavily on a well-balanced, vitamin-enriched diet.

Okay, get out that pencil and let's get started.

1. How, exactly, do they get the whipped cream in the middle of a Hostess cupcake?

a) First, they get the whipped cream and build the cupcake around it.
b) They grow them this way, using the same technique as for seedless oranges, only in reverse.
c) It's magic.
d) I know the answer, but if I told you, I'd have to kill you.

ANSWER: The correct response is (d). How the whipped cream gets into the cupcake is a closely guarded military secret. For $10, however, we *will* tell you the secret herbs and spices used for Kentucky Fried Chicken.

2. *Of the following, which one is really NOT a fruit: Froot Loops, Fruit Roll-ups, Juicy Fruit, tomato, Fruit By The Foot, Super Fruity Kool-Aid, Fruitopia.*
a) Fruit Roll-ups.
b) Froot Loops.
c) Fruit By The Foot.
d) tomato.

ANSWER: If you picked (d), you are correct. The tomato is a vegetable. We think. We might have to get back to you on this one.

3. *How much do you save if you buy the McDonald's Extra-Value Meal, as opposed to buying the sandwich, fries, and drink separately?*
a) 40 cents.
b) 75 cents.
c) 95 cents.
d) You save nothing, but the government saves two weeks of your Old Age Pension for each meal you consume after the age of 40.

ANSWER: Once again, it's (d). A steady diet of these not only reduces the demand on social services from that aging population, but helps heart surgeons maintain their BMW payments.

4. Your child is demanding a bowl of ice cream for dessert, but has already eaten today a McCain's Deep'n delicious chocolate cake, 15 Freezies, a box of Girl Guide cookies (even the vanilla side), and, at the afternoon showing of Free Willy 5: The Whale Takes Manhattan, a tub of popcorn with enough butter on it to send the entire population of Lindsay, Ontario, into cardiac arrest. What do you say?
   a) No.
   b) Okay, but NO sprinkles.

ANSWER: The obvious response is, of course, (b). Compromise and moderation go hand in hand in these matters.

5. Breakfast is the most important meal of the day. Which of the following combinations offer the most balanced approach for your youngster?
   a) Orange juice, shredded wheat with milk, grapefruit.
   b) Grape juice, All-Bran with sliced banana, or oatmeal.
   c) Apple juice, lightly buttered toast with peanut butter, cantaloupe.
   d) Count Chocula, frozen waffles with artificial maple syrup, Frosted Pop Tarts, Trix, and a frothy cup of cappuccino.

ANSWER: Like you didn't know. It's (d), because there's nothing like a cup of cappuccino to make a child feel *so* grown up. And it's the perfect thing to warm him up when he's facing a cold, wintry walk to school. Just remember to go easy on the chocolate shavings; you don't want to make him sick.

Scoring: So how'd you do? If you scored a perfect 5, chances are you're the kind of dad who leads by example, which is exactly why you had that third piece of carrot cake the other night. You understand the importance of eating your vegetables.

The Children's Menu

Children are extremely reluctant to try anything new. You would think, with the number of times North Americans eat out of the home in a given week, that kids would be exposed to new taste sensations on a regular basis, but they aren't because of what is known as "The Children's Menu."

Until a child is at least 12, he will be unaware of any other kind of food than Pizza, The Hot Dog, or The Chicken Nugget. There is nothing else.

In fact, these are not technically foods at all, but food substitutes that parents are willing to let their children eat so that they, the grown-ups, can have a treat and be freed from the hassle of making dinner at home, where, if they'd stayed, they would have made their kid pizza, a hot dog, or some chicken nuggets.

But to be fair, a lot of thought does go into the typical child's menu. Restaurant managers, concerned that *all* their patrons, not just the adults, be served nothing but the finest fare, spend hours trying to come up with just the right kiddies' menu.

For example: Should it have a word-search game? A "what's-wrong-with-this-picture?" puzzle? Connect the dots?

A few restaurants have experimented with children's menus that feature Sesame Chicken with Green Peppers and Walnut Sauce, Brown Rice with Dill and Cucumber Beef, or Swordfish with Mustard Sauce.

Those that have gone this route are now closed, and are getting ready to reopen under the name "Bob's Deep-Fried Wiener."

Not only do children hate to try anything different, but even the most minor variation in one of their favorite foods can send them into fits of despair, as the following chart indicates.

How a child's favorite food can be completely destroyed

Ingredients of pizza #1, prepared perfectly	Ingredients of pizza #2, rendered totally inedible
double cheese	double cheese
pepperoni	pepperoni
pineapple	pineapple
sausage	sausage
	one infinitesimally small bit of mushroom, not visible to the naked adult eye and detectable only through the aid of a neutron miscroscope, that fell off the pizza that was being made next to this one

Timing

There are two basic rules concerning a child's appetite:
1. He will not be hungry when it is time for him to be fed.
2. He will be starving when it is *not* time for anyone to even be THINKING of preparing a meal.

Scene One:

Dad: Okay, I've made your favorite! Spaghetti and meatballs with the shaky cheese on top and would you believe it! Strawberry Jell-O for dessert!

Child: I'm not hungry.

Scene Two, six hours later:

Wife: You know how I've been having all these headaches this past week?

23

Husband: (warily) Yes.

Wife: Well, I am definitely, positively, NOT having a headache tonight, big fella.

Child: (in doorway) I'm hungry. Could you please put some of those frozen potato puffs in the oven for me? They only take half an hour.

Packing Your Child's School Lunch

The important thing to keep in mind when preparing a meal that will be consumed outside the home is striking a comfortable balance between fat and sugar. Some children may want their lunch box filled with nothing but slices of pepperoni, cheese, and potato chips, but you have to be firm with them. "Listen here, buster," you must say, "you're also taking cookies and a pudding cup."

Your child may attend a school that stresses, in its curriculum, the importance of a nutritious diet. If this is the case for you, well, you have our sympathies.

But unless you're prepared to pack up your family and move to a place where no one, not the schools, not even the government's health ministry, cares how badly the population eats (we are speaking, of course, of England, where, on any given night most people dine on a delicacy known as Lard and Chips), then you're just going to have to adjust.

A school like this can especially be a pain if the teachers, who are basically snoops, take an interest in what students are bringing for lunch. Now you run the risk of your child's teacher actually taking a peek at what you've packed in that lunch box.

Grade school teachers, who are awfully serious about such things as diet and nutrition and the ozone layer and recycling and treating everyone with respect, aren't likely to be terribly amused when they see that the closest thing to a vegetable your child has in his lunch box is some grass, which only got there after he had to repack his lunch after spilling it on the playground.

Many parents try putting fruit in their kids' lunches, but this has met with limited success. An uneaten piece of fruit discovered at the end of the day is often just left there by parents in the hopes that it will be eaten at the *next* lunch time.

This means that a single, shiny McIntosh can often cover more territory in a week than a Hyundai Sonata commuting daily between Hamilton and Toronto.

You soon realize that the apple is not there for your child, but for the teacher. And this has nothing to do with the old tradition of placing an apple on the teacher's desk to score brownie points. The apple stays in the lunch box to indicate to school staff that you care enough about your child's nutrition to pack him a piece of fruit every single day.

After a few days, however, this apple begins to look bruised and wrinkly and pretty much unappetizing. If it's STILL in your child's lunch box in this condition when the teacher conducts her inspection, the principal will be brought in, and then the school nurse, and then a call will be put in to the child welfare authorities, and, finally, the science teacher, who will use the apple to start a worm farm. (If you use a banana instead of an apple, you can expect this whole process to begin no later than the second day.)

> **Five Interesting Ways
> to Serve Your Child
> Kraft Dinner**
> ☆
> In a Lion King dish
> In an Aladdin dish
> In a Little Mermaid dish
> In a Pocahontas dish
> In a Beauty and the Beast dish

The perfect solution: Consider investing in a small wax fruit collection.

Just throw in a piece of imitation fruit in your kid's lunch. A fake orange, banana, or apple will last for days and look reasonably convincing to school authorities.

About the only thing you need to worry about here is The Trade. There is a chance, though remote, that somewhere in your child's school there is *one* kid, one healthy, rosy-cheeked, flaxen-haired child, who has his own health club membership at age nine and *actually likes fruit.*

One day, your kid will happen to eat his lunch next to this child, and the following conversation will ensue.

Healthy child: Wow, that's a very nutritious-looking bunch of grapes you have there.

Your child: Yeah, they've been there for four weeks now and they never go bad.

Healthy child: Wanna trade?

Your child: Whattya got?

Healthy child: Uh, I got Robocop Rice Cakes, Ninja Turtle Wheat Germ, and some Terminator Tofu.

Your child: Where does it say all that?

Healthy child: Well, that's what my parents call it. They say they just remove the labels before packing it so other kids won't steal it from me.

Your child: Cool! I'll give you my grapes for some of that Terminator Tofu!

Healthy child: Deal! *(some serious chewing ensues)* Boy, these are sure fresh! They've got quite a crunch to them, although they remind me a bit of my wax monster lips I wore at Halloween. How's the Terminator Tofu?

Your child: Medic!

4

Teaching Kids Manners

(Or: Discouraging children from using food for purposes other than eating)

You can never begin too early to teach children the importance of good manners.

This is a tremendous responsibility for parents, and fathers must take an active role. Their children will be judged throughout their lives on how well they present themselves. Their very careers, their success in social situations, all can hinge on how insistent their parents were at hammering "please" and "thank you" into their heads.

There is also the added consideration that when you send your children out into the world, or even to one of their friends' houses for a sleepover, YOU will be judged by how your children behave. The last thing you want is all the other parents in the neighborhood saying to each other: "Haven't they taught their kids ANYTHING?"

Now, we would, of course, hate to make any sweeping generalizations, but many fathers are less knowledgeable in the area of social niceties than mothers. Okay, maybe "many" is a bit unfair. What we really mean to say is "all."

27

When presented with a finger bowl for the first time, many dads will drink it. They may even eat the piece of lemon. When introduced to a spouse's coworker, many will not realize that "Hey, when my wife said you were stacked, she wasn't kidding" is an inappropriate form of greeting. Many new husbands will not be aware that the sending of thank-you notes for wedding gifts should be undertaken before the celebration of the silver anniversary.

So you see, many children who desperately need reminders about the importance of good manners from BOTH parents can start life with a distinct disadvantage if their father is the kind of person who thinks that if you've got a sleeve handy, what's the point of hunting around for a tissue?

But once they become parents, men MUST make an effort to get with the program. And they must do it quickly, especially when you consider that even young children can end up being invited to important social events, like weddings, anniversaries, bar mitzvahs, and Super Bowl parties.

It's a real plus if they're familiar with the social graces.

Dad: Now, let's go over this one more time. This one is the salad fork, this is the dinner fork, this is the dessert spoon, and this is the spoon you use for your tea or coffee. At least, I THINK that's the salad fork. Or is that one of those ones you use to get olives out of the jar? It might actually be a back-scratcher, or an extremely elegant shoehorn. Let's just see here . . . *YOUCHH!* Nope, not a shoehorn. And remember, when you're eating soup, you take your spoonful from the far edge, don't blow on it so hard that it creates waves, and never slurp when you're drinking that last little bit out of the bowl. Have you got all that?

Child: Ga ga momma boof boof.

Becoming more mannerly can sometimes cramp a sophisticated father's sense of humor.

For example, for years this author, when he really wants to gross out his wife, takes a couple of huge bites of banana, chews them up pretty well, then opens his mouth wide, putting this masticated masterpiece on display.

Husband Humor doesn't get any better than this, but if you maintain this high level of comedic brilliance once you have children, you run the risk of your kids doing the same thing, but instead of bananas, they'll use strained peas, mashed carrots, and liquefied chicken, which is not, let's face it, the *least* bit funny, but just plain disgusting.

Nagging Your Children Senseless

Where manners are concerned, you must never let up, otherwise children will fall back into bad habits. You must correct them relentlessly.

You'll know you've done a good job here when, upon asking your child how his day at school went, he blurts out: "Yes, PLEASE! I mean, THANK YOU! I mean, whatever you're serving is just fine with me!"

Often, a child knows the importance of saying "thank you," but just needs a little help, a little *reminder* to say the right thing, like when you pick your daughter up after she's spent a day with her best friend Emily and her mother and father.

Dad: Susie, do you have anything to say to Mr. and Mrs. Dweebleheimer for taking you to Disney World, the air show, the Planet Hollywood restaurant in Manhattan for dinner, and a behind-the-scenes tour of the *Ace Ventura Part IV* movie set?

Susie: Huh?

Dad: (clearing his throat angrily) Susie? Are you SURE you don't have something to say to these wonderful, nice people?

Susie: No, not really.

Dad: ARE YOU ABSOLUTELY SURE?

Susie: Oh yeah. Right! I almost forgot. Mr. and Mrs. Dweebleheimer, you said we'd get to meet Jim Carrey. He wasn't there. You

PROMISED that he was going to be there. I told all my FRIENDS I was gonna get to meet Jim Carrey. Where do you guys get off building up a child's expectations like that and then not coming across?

Dad: (cheerily) And maybe we can return the favor and have Emily over to OUR house for the day!

At the Dinner Table

It's at the dinner table where good manners really shine. A child who conducts himself appropriately through a meal leaves adults with an excellent impression.

If your family is going to someone else's house for dinner, whether it's the grandparents or in-laws or just good friends, you want your children to know how to behave.

Here are the basic rules to instill in your youngsters.

1. Take small bites: Many children eat in such a way as to give the impression that they may have served some time in a correctional facility, or, at the very least, been raised by wolves.

    If a kid is able to consume two cheeseburgers, a Coke, three bags of all-dressed chips, a popsicle, and an entire sleeve of President's Choice Decadent Chocolate Chip Cookies, all in under 20 seconds, you know this is a kid who's worried about finishing off his meal before anyone else, or any member of the wildebeest family, can get a crack at it.

    This is the kind of child who can stuff so much in his mouth at once that you want to get him a guest shot on Letterman doing a Dizzy Gillespie impression, except the moment he attempts to blow the trumpet, $93 worth of groceries will suddenly appear, in a not-terribly appetizing condition, on national television.

    Children who can eat both sides of a sandwich simultaneously must be taught to take smaller bites, particularly when they're at someone else's house. There are few greater faux pas than having the host dive in to perform the Heimlich maneuver on your child. (If this does happen, be aware that Miss Manners says you should at least OFFER to clean up the resulting mess.)

2. Ask permission to leave the table: You can spot a kid with no breeding a mile away. (That's 1.6 kilometers for you folks from Celsiusburg.) He's the one who, once he's finished eating, pushes himself away from the table and runs outside to play with his friends, all without saying a word.

   But a child who's from a family where good manners are stressed is the one you can always count on to say: "Pardon me, but may I please be excused from the table, because there's simply no way I can gag down another bite of this swill."

3. Never play with food, nor use it as weaponry: This is one that can't be stressed enough. How many times have you heard those OTHER parents, out for dinner with their kids at the food court in the mall, scream: "Stop stabbing your brother with that French fry right this instant! What do you think the plastic knives are for?"

   The only possible exception here might be the Brussels sprout, which, as anyone who's ever eaten one knows, tastes so unbelievably disgusting that it must have been dreamed up by Mother Nature on one of her off days, probably the same day when she came up with rutabaga.

   An *uncooked* Brussels sprout, however, is quite hard and its nearly spherical shape makes it ideal for beaning someone in the head.

   Children should also be discouraged from molding their mashed potatoes into replicas of mountain ranges, alien faces, or body parts that no one ever wants to think about while eating, let alone find represented on their plate.

   You might consider an exception, however, if you're the father of a gifted child who can use his mashed potatoes to recreate, right down to the most subtle grade variations, the 14th green at the Glen Abbey Golf and Country Club. With a single garden pea, you should be able to gain some insights into why your ball's always been breaking to the left.

Interrupting

Children must be taught that it is rude to interrupt adults when they are speaking, especially when grown-ups are involved in intense conversations of a very sensitive nature.

Dad #1: Okay, give me a minute, I'm CERTAIN I can name all the superheroes who were in the Justice League of America. I had ALL those comics when I was a kid. There was Superman, of course, and —

Child: Dad —

Dad #2: Hey, can't you see that Mr. Fitzwiller and I are having a conversation here? So you say Superman, Bill? Anybody would know that, sheesh.

Dad #1: And Batman, and there was Wonder Woman, I think, and there was the guy in the green costume, not Hornet, but Green —

Child: But Daaaadd —

Dad #2: What did I just tell you, son? Okay, Bill, I'll give you that one, since you almost got it. It was Green Lantern, but there was also —

Child: Daaaad, Sparky's in —

Dad #2: We are TALKING here! Can't you see that? We are having a grown-up, adult discussion about some very important matters, but when we are FINISHED, I'd be happy to listen to what you have to say.

Dad #1: Was Atom one of them? And Flash? I really loved Flash. Boy, could he ever run fast, huh? And what about Hawkeye?

Child: Dad, Sparky just puked in the Volvo.

Finally

Just because a child has excellent manners does not necessarily mean he's a terrific kid. Some children exhibit signs of Eddie Haskell Syndrome, named after the *Leave It to Beaver* character who was totally charming with the Beav's mother, but wouldn't think twice about ripping out the differential from under Lumpy's car.

But to be pragmatic about it, given a choice between a totally amoral child with terrific manners, and a totally amoral child with chocolate smeared around his mouth who talks with his mouth full, you know which way you're better off — especially if you just got new furniture for the family room.

5

Sex

(Or: "We have sex almost every night. We almost had it Monday, we almost had it Tuesday, we almost had it Wednesday . . .")

Most times, when you mention the word "sex" to parents, they immediately start looking for little boxes marked "m" or "f."

That's because the only time they see this word is on those boxes that show up on forms for summer school, children's insurance, and swimming lesson registrations. These vitally important forms come daily into the home, where they are stuck into a drawer to be dealt with immediately and not remembered until the child starts college.

"No, no," you say. "We're not talking about that kind of sex, we are talking about the *other* kind of sex."

It is necessary to be patient with parents at times like these, as they give you blank stares, like you are one of their children's computer games that they could no more explain than tell you where elephants go to die.

"Ohhhhhh," they will finally nod. "You mean like on *Beverly Hills 90210*. Or on some of those videos the kids like to watch on the rock station. Oh yes, we know what you're talking about, and we're doing everything we can to stamp it out."

Perhaps at this point you'd rather go to your local highway improvement store, stick your head in a medium-sized metal culvert, and direct someone to strike it as hard as possible with a sledgehammer. But you must persist.

"No," you say, grasping this couple by the collars and giving them a few gentle slaps, "we are talking about YOU. How is YOUR sex life?"

Well, that's something different altogether. The average parents will have vague recollections of sex mainly because there are daily reminders of the penalties of sex walking around the house, sticking their heads into the fridge every five minutes, putting toothbrushes into the toilet and thereby requiring the services of a plumber for the reasonable price of $172.34 an hour, and trying to dress up the schnauzer in Cabbage Patch doll clothes.

Once they actually have their children, parents are neither expected nor entitled to have sex. After all, they've already had some, and they need to leave some for other people.

But noted marriage counselors and therapists (all of whom are single, drive Porsches, get paid a fortune to dispense useless advice on Oprah, and don't have to get up early Saturday morning for T-ball) will tell you that having children doesn't have to mean the end of a healthy, fulfilling, and mutually satisfying sex life.

"Parents," they say, "must treat themselves. They must not take each other for granted. They must set aside time to be alone, even if that means arranging a date later in the week. Set that special time, and stick to it."

If you believe this is possible, you might be interested in some swampland the author is selling.

Arranging That Special Date

Picture the following scene:

A wife sidles up to her husband in the kitchen while the kids play down the hall.

Wife: Hey, you stud muffin you, I think it's time you and I had a little time together.

Husband: Have you seen my socket wrenches?

Wife: I've got just the socket for you, Tool Man.

Husband: I looked for them in the garage, and I looked in the basement, and I don't think Herb next door borrowed them. So just WHERE THE HECK DO YOU THINK THEY COULD BE?

Wife: (slipping hand behind belt at the front of his pants) Hmmmmm.

Husband: Well surely you don't think I'd have left them down there, do you?

Wife: I want you, you fool.

Husband: (finally getting the drift) Honey! The kids are just down the hall!

Wife: Not now, but tomorrow night, after the kids are in bed — 10 o'clock sharp, meet me in the bubble bath. Bring the candles.

Children's Sonar

Children are born with several instinctive needs. Chief among these are the desire for love and parental approval. And, especially, the need for attention. As we discussed in an earlier chapter, they do not want to share this attention with other siblings, so instinctively they will do whatever it takes to ensure that no more siblings come along.

That's why children are born with an uncanny ability to predict when their parents are planning to have sex. The children do not even KNOW that they know their parents have arranged a rendez-vous in the sack, but they pick up on subtle signals that love is in the air.

Like when their father says: "I want you kids in bed on time tonight, no IFS, ANDS, OR BUTS!!!" This is a very good clue.

Upon hearing this, the child's automatic defense mechanism system kicks in.

So when the couple you met earlier finally settle down for their romantic evening, it goes like this:

8:30 p.m.: Daughter is told that this, absolutely, positively, is "lights out" time. She MUST get a good sleep, she's told, because tomorrow is a very busy day.

8:37 p.m.: Mother and father close their own bedroom door, start getting ready for bed, brushing teeth, etc.

8:45 p.m.: Knock at the door. Child says there is a monster in her closet.

8:45–9:10 p.m.: Both parents try to persuade their daughter that there really is NOT a monster in her closet by opening the door and taking out all her shoes and all the clothes off the rack and all the toys she never plays with off the top shelf. Once the closet is totally empty, the daughter says: "Then the noise I heard must have been from the attic."

9:11 p.m.: Parents' preparations for bedtime resume. Door is no sooner closed than there is another knock. Child says there is a spider in her room.

9:15 p.m.: Father, with the aid of a magnifying glass, has been able to identify spider on wall. Catches it with tissue, tucks daughter into bed.

9:22 p.m.: Parents' bedroom door is closed again, deadbolted, and dresser dragged across it. Father brushes teeth. Mother gets under the covers, starts asking him questions from latest *Cosmo* quiz, "Would Your Husband Make a Good Love Slave?"

9:31 p.m.: Knock at the door.

9:32 p.m.: Once dresser is moved away and door opened, child says: "Friday is Blue Jay Baseball Day at school and I have to wear something to school that's about the Blue Jays." Mother says: "I don't think you have anything with the Blue Jays on it." Child says: "But I HAVE to wear something with the Blue Jays on it because it's Blue Jay day and everyone is going to be wearing something with a Blue Jay on it and I can't be the only one to wear something that doesn't have a Blue Jay on it!" Mother says: "Okay, okay, we'll find something. But let's talk about it in the morning." Child asks: "What are you reading?"

9:40 p.m.: Daughter is tucked back into bed, parents' bedroom door is again secured, this time with the aid of a board, hammer, and nails. Father gets under the covers. Mother points to article in *Cosmo* and says: "Oh my God, there's the neatest idea here. Run down to the fridge and get the grape jelly." Knock at the door.

9:41 p.m.: "Do you love me?"

9:45 p.m.: Father reads daughter first five chapters of *The Secret Garden*.

10:37 p.m.: He returns to their bedroom, announces with great satisfaction "She's asleep!" but is drowned out by the mother's snoring.

10:38 p.m.: Mother wakes up, says YES, of COURSE she's still interested, the night is still young, it doesn't matter that she has a 7:30 meeting the next morning, you wonderful hunk of man, you, let her just wipe the sleep out of her eye.

10:41 p.m.: Knock at the door. "My stomach feels funny, would it be okay if I slept with you guys?"

Telepathic Sex

Sometimes the only recourse for parents who would like to be sexually active, if they could remember what exactly that means, is what has come to be known as Telepathic Sex.

It works like this: Your wife is still in your bed, next to a youngster who has finally fallen asleep after complaining of cramps, the cause of which was a complete mystery, because after all, she felt just great when she was eating those 29 strawberries dipped in chocolate.

You, however, have decided to sack out in your daughter's room. But you can still communicate through intense thought patterns with your mate. If you both think of each other in an intimate, sensual way, you can achieve a kind of spiritual, karma-like coupling that, while perhaps not as satisfying as the real thing, doesn't get you all sweaty.

Some men may have some trouble getting used to this, as their erotic thoughts are often interrupted by internal debates over the designated hitter rule, whether the Leafs have got a chance this year, and if it's GREEN kryptonite or RED kryptonite that can kill Superman.

The Dirty Weekend

Many parents find getting away by themselves for a couple of days is the only way to keep the passion alive.

This is not impossible. Sometimes you can work a deal with friends who have children of their own. If they'll look after your kids for a couple of nights, you tell them, then when they want to get away for a weekend, you'll return the favor.

The important thing to remember here is make sure you get your weekend away first. That way, when you renege on the deal because the last thing in the world you want is to have to look after their two little hellraisers, you'll at least have had your time away on your own.

If you don't have friends or relatives to leave the kids with, consider hiring a babysitter who's trained in watching over kids for more than just an evening.

The best way to determine whether the sitter is suited for the job is a thorough interrogation. Something like the following.

Parent: Now, are you fully qualified to look after two demanding children, to give them baths, to read them a story and tuck them in at night, and make them a healthy breakfast and lunch and dinner, and make sure they don't get into any kind of trouble? To be nurturing, and fair, and demonstrate the kind of wisdom that all great parents hold? Are you SURE you're able to take on all that?

Sitter: (snapping her gum) Yeah, well, gee, I don't know, mayb—

Parent: Great, then, you're hired.

Now all you have to do is make reservations at your favorite hotel, fill the suitcase with lotions, sexy lingerie, unbelievably dirty reading material (anything by Judith Krantz), and engage in some of the most disgusting, repulsive, outlawed-in-10-provinces, wonderful kind of sex imaginable.

Or, if you prefer, you can do what most couples do: sleep.

If you could see what actually goes on behind the closed doors of a hotel room that is occupied by a married couple away without their children, this is what you would find: Unpacked suitcases dropped on the floor and two people, fully clothed, face down on the covers, their feet, still with shoes on, sticking out over the end of the bed, as though the two of them had fallen there and could not get up.

Sometimes, hotel maids will mistakenly walk in on a scene like this and call the front desk: "I think we have a murder–suicide in 402."

The couple will remain in this position until it is time to go home, where they will report that they have had the best vacation of their entire lives.

Answering Your Child's Questions About Sex

When should you explain the facts of life to children?

Are children entitled to know the whole story once they begin to ask questions? Will you adopt the attitude that sex is a wonderful, beautiful, perfectly normal, and healthy thing, the filthy details of which should not be divulged until after the kids have graduated from college?

And what do you do if a child who may not yet be ready for all the facts finds that stash of *Playboy* magazines you've held onto since your wild and crazy single days, because you thought someday you might need to refer to some of those terrific articles they ran?[1]

Regrettably, television is a major factor in deciding when to give your children more information. Because even general audience programs are dealing with sexual matters in a more frank and straightforward manner (e.g., that episode of *Theodore Tugboat* where the fishing boat decides, after much counseling, to have an operation making it into a Land Rover), don't be surprised if your child comes to you with any one of the following questions.

1. Where do babies come from?
2. Why do boys and girls like to kiss each other?
3. When will I have cleavage?
4. Why does Lois Lane always seem to be short of breath when

---

[1]Yes there are also ARTICLES in *Playboy*.

41

Superman's carrying her around? Is it just because the air's thin up there?

5. What chances do you give a relationship between a transsexual hooker and a man whose gender role has been confused because he was forced to wear dresses when he was little?

Now, this last question is most likely to come from children who have been home sick for the day and have spent it in bed watching the talk shows. Or, if they aren't home sick, they're racing home to watch television once school is over.

Children get away with watching these kinds of shows because, after school, many parents are too consumed with other duties. Struggling to make dinner, they are constantly having to stop what they're doing to answer the phone to respond to telemarketers' surveys THAT WILL ONLY TAKE TWO MINUTES.

When parents are under this kind of stress, they ignore everything they've always thought they believed in ("Oh, we STRICTLY monitor what they watch on television, we're VERY concerned about THAT") and plunk their kids down in front of the tube so they can start boiling water for spaghetti.

That's why today it's more likely that before children learn about the sperm and the egg, they will have a full understanding of the issues surrounding sexually transmitted diseases, transvestism, gay rights, inadequacy, sexual addiction, men who fool around with their wives' sisters, women who cheat with their husbands' fathers, guys who've slept with their girlfriends' therapists, mothers who don't want their daughters to be prostitutes, men who think their girlfriends dress too sexy, women who think their mothers dress too sexy, sons and daughters who think their parents dress like farmers, and nuns who strip to draw attention to their campaign against photo radar.

This can make things somewhat difficult for parents, most of whom are unable to keep up with the latest sexual trends because they are too busy making a living to watch talk shows.

So today, responsible parents, before they leave for work and drop off their kids at school in the morning, set up their VCRs to tape *Montel, Oprah, Ricki Lake, Jenny Jones, Jerry Springer, Donahue,* and *Geraldo.* It also helps to watch, in the evenings, *Melrose Place, Baywatch,* and *Married with Children.*

Since this is where children are getting all their information on sex, a parent has got to keep up.

6

All About Money

(Or: When your kid's lemonade stand files for bankruptcy)

The first thing any good father must learn before he can teach his own children the fine details of money management is how to harangue them, in a general sense, about how much things cost. Commit to memory the following.

Ten really original things dads like to say about issues involving money

1. "Have you confused me with Donald Trump?"
2. "You want a BOOK? You already HAVE a book."
3. "Did some rich uncle of yours die without me knowing about it?"
4. "You want money? Get a job."
5. "All I ever got for an allowance was 25 cents."
6. "You can have a drink when we get home."

7. "Do you think money grows on trees?"
8. "You ever hear of the Depression?"
9. "Hey! Who turned up the heat?"
10. "Hey! Who turned on the air?"

Make sure you know these by heart before reading any further. These phrases constitute the Father's Economic Manifesto. They are the cornerstone of your beliefs. They don't matter a whit, and they'll be broken down on a daily basis, but it's comforting to repeat them once in a while, even if no one is listening.

Where Does Money Come From?

When we were kids, it gradually dawned on us that money was a reward, something that came from hard work, something you got after you first expended a little blood, sweat, and tears.

Today children deduce — even before they can say the word "credit" — that money comes from machines. You can find these machines just about any place. There are machines at the mall, machines at the grocery store, even machines at drive-through locations where all parents have to do is put down the window and slide in their card to load up on wads of cash.

You can even find these machines at banks, where, thank heavens, they have replaced people, who were always making the banking experience so intrusive by addressing you by your actual name and asking things like how you were and how old your daughter was and wishing you stuff like Merry Christmas and Happy New Year.

For kids today, the message is clear: "I gotta get me one of those cards."

Cards are to today's children what the story of Aladdin's lamp was to us when we were young. But who needs three lousy wishes when you've got a bank card?

The challenge is to make your children understand how the money actually gets there; that you STILL must have a job, and that

45

you must work very, very hard (unless you are, for example, a newspaper columnist), for there to be any cash in that machine when you put your card in.

"Okay," says the child, "but how did they know you were going to THAT machine?"

Setting Up an Allowance

Once a child has a vague understanding of money, say something on the level of a federal finance minister, you may want to start her out on a weekly allowance.

Just how much this should be depends on several factors, including the child's age, what her friends receive, where you live, and whether you are the president of Microsoft or the evil dictator of a small, impoverished country. (If it's the former, something in the low six figures will probably strike you as about right, but if the latter, you can skip an allowance altogether and just take your little princess to the home of one of your loyal subjects and shake him down for a little cash.)

You want to give her enough money that she'll be able to buy some of the things she wants, but not everything. This will automatically teach her the value of saving some of her money, which she'll keep in a little Minnie Mouse purse up in her room.

A thrifty child can accumulate a bundle of money in a hurry. Make sure you know where this is, because one day you're going to order a double-cheese, thin-crust with extra hot peppers from Domino's and discover when it arrives that neither you nor your wife have 10 cents between you.

At this point you'll tell the delivery man to hang on a second while you rifle through your daughter's purse and learn that not only has she been saving her allowances, but clearly has been extorting lunch money from classmates.

It is difficult at times like these to know whether to be concerned or proud.

When Kids Want More Money

Before long, children will conclude that their allowance is too low. They will start trying to negotiate a larger one.

"What if," your seven-year-old daughter says, "I did some things around the house to help out? Could I get some more money then?"

Well, you explain, we're a FAMILY here, and that means we all pitch in and do chores without being paid, like Daddy doesn't get paid to make dinner or drive you to school or help you with your homework, blah, blah, blah, yadda, yadda, yadda.

BUT, you continue, thinking that this is not only an opportunity to teach your daughter some financial responsibility, but a chance to scratch a few things off that list of household projects you haven't had time to get to, there just might be a few things she could do to earn an extra buck or two.

Just be sure she's familiar enough with the safe operation of power tools before you have her replace the linoleum in the kitchen, put on an addition, or change the oil in your Bonneville.

If she's not satisfied with doing these simple types of household duties, however, she may want to go into business for herself.

A terrific introduction to the world of commerce is the lemonade stand.

Get her all set up at the end of the driveway, and once she's experienced the thrill of waiting on customers and of running her very own business, sit down and share with her all the things this new experience has taught her.

Then give her the following statement.

47

The lemonade stand: annual report

Income	Expenses	Profit
30 cups of lemonade @ 25 cents each	30 plastic cups, 5 containers frozen lemonade, rental of small table, chair, sign production costs, end-of-driveway leasing arrangement, local Business Improvement Area fees, insurance, business license, protection money to neighborhood enforcer	
Total = $7.50	$234.89	−$227.39

Not only is this a terrific lesson for your child in how the real world operates, but it means she owes you more than 200 big ones. That means no allowance for over a year, and that doesn't even count the interest.

Household Finances:
What Should the Kids Know?

Personal finances are, well, very personal.

Do you want your children to know how much money you make, how much you paid for your house, how big your mortgage is, how much money you've borrowed from your parents?

Consider the following exchange.

Son: Dad, how much money do you make?

Dad: Well, son, what I make, and what your mother makes, is more than enough to provide for all of us. Grown-ups don't go around bragging about what they make, not to their kids or their friends, either. It's a much more mature approach.

Son: Rodney told me what HIS dad makes.

Dad: Rodney told you what Mr. Quigley makes?

Son: Yup.

Dad: Well. Isn't that interesting. How, uh, much did he say his dad makes, exactly?

Son: He said he's rakin' in about $84,000 a year.

Dad: Get out.

Son: Really, that's what he said. And they've got a boat, and they go to Florida every winter for two weeks.

Dad: He's a cable installer.

Son: Yeah. I guess they do a lot better than accountants, huh, Dad?

Dad: Now, son, I would never want you to repeat this to anyone outside the house *(nudge nudge, wink wink)*, but Daddy makes, uh, lots more than Mr. Quigley. Oh, maybe $10,000 more.

Son: (all agog) Really?

Dad: Now, this doesn't make Daddy any better than Mr. Quigley, well, not a LOT better. Listen, you run along now, maybe give your friend Rodney a call. *(Child leaves.)* Marge, get in here, I've got something to tell you!

When you're going through tough times financially, should you shield the children from the situation or should you fill them in on what's going on, teach them that when a family faces a problem together, it makes them stronger?

When you and your spouse are sitting around the kitchen table late at night, trying to balance the checkbook, scribbling figures on scraps of paper, and sniping at one another, children are going to notice.

Daughter: What's going on with you guys? Are you fighting?

Dad: No, sweetheart. We're just trying to figure out how much money we've got. Now, I know you're only six years old, and this will be hard for you to understand, but sometimes Mommy and

Daddy have lots of bills that add up to more money than we make. Do you understand what that means?

Daughter: Sure. You're running in the red. Your cards are maxxed to the limit, you can't even make the minimum monthly balance, and every time anyone else sends you a credit card you go ahead and use it when you should be cutting it up into little pieces. You bought a Harley-Davidson while we're eating Kraft Dinner, spent half your paycheck on Miller Lite, and if you've got a scrap of sense left you'll see a credit counselor first thing in the morning.

Dad: Well, maybe your mother can explain it to you.

7

Signing Your Kids Up for Things

(Or: You have to run all over town, but there's always the chance you can run some Norwegian mime artists into the ditch)

There was a time, when kids came home from school, that their schedule was something like this:

4:00 p.m.: Arrive home, have some milk and cookies.

4:30 p.m.: Watch *Rocky and Bullwinkle.*

5:00 p.m.: Run around outside; play with friends down the street; ride banana-seat bike helmetless around the neighborhood; jump off ramps made with planks and concrete blocks.

6:00 p.m.: Come in and inhale dinner.

6:02 p.m.: Race back outside and play some more. Get horrible cramps from running after eating two Shake 'n Bake chicken breasts and macaroni and cheese. Hide out from girls in buddy's treehouse, until it starts to get dark, and then let them in. Yee-ha!

8:00 p.m.: Fight with parents about whether a bath is needed. Lose fight, have bath. If there's time, watch the end of *The Time Tunnel.*

9:00 p.m.: Go to bed, turn off light.

9:07 p.m.: As soon as parents go downstairs, turn on small bedside lamp and read dirty parts again from parents' copy of *The Godfather* by Mario Puzo.

10:35 p.m.: Fall asleep.

But things are a bit different today.

Now that we are parents ourselves, we've concluded that our mothers and fathers were totally out of their minds to allow us all that free time. We still remember quite clearly what we were up to.

When we weren't playing out front of the house with our friends, we were exploring storm drains, sneaking into houses still under construction, scaling trees to see if we could actually reach the hydro wires, grabbing onto the tailfins of moving cars while we rode our bikes, strolling down railroad tracks and running to get across trestles before the train came, trying to dam the local creek, knocking on people's doors and then hiding in the bushes, setting off landslides in the local gravel pit, exploring abandoned warehouses, phoning the butcher to see if he had pigs' feet,[1] and whittling. Whittling was big. A stick or a branch and a good sharp knife and you were talking major entertainment.

We were having the time of our lives, and endangering them every step of the way.

So, as a way of exerting more control over our own children's free time, today's generation of parents have opted to enrol their kids in the odd after-school activity.

These programs do more than enrich our children and expand their horizons. They ensure that from the time school ends to the time children are tucked in at night, the highways of the nation are clogged with fleets of cars and minivans driven by parents who are mainlining coffee and coming to view operators of fast-food

---

[1] "Keep your shoes on and we won't tell anyone!"

drive-through windows as members of their family.

What follows is the after-school schedule of a typical suburban family, where the dad, home early from work, is today's designated chauffeur.

It goes something like this:

4:00 p.m.: Brother and sister arrive home from school. Father screams: "Eat this snack! Come on! Eat it now! How was school today? Great! Glad to hear it!"

To the daughter: "Ballet class starts in 20 minutes, so let's move it! As soon as you finish get your leotard and put your bag by the front door! CHECK THAT YOU HAVE YOUR SHOES THIS TIME! And make sure you've got your bathing suit! And don't forget your other things!"

To the son: "As soon as I drop her off at ballet I'll drop you off at soccer practice. EAT! Chew! Chew! You can't play hard on an empty stomach! Come on, come on, let's go! And PLEASE remember that this is your first day for wrestling, so let's get going!"

4:10 p.m.: Daughter, rummaging through her ballet case in back-seat, says: "Mom didn't put the ribbons on my ballet slippers. She PROMISED she would put the ribbons on my ballet slippers. How can I go in there today without ribbons?"

Father, narrowly avoiding another van driven by a mother taking her kids to swimming and band lessons, says he doesn't know anything about ribbons, he doesn't CARE anything about ribbons, but if it's REALLY important, he has his toolbox in the back and can staple-gun them on.

4:15 p.m.: Father drops daughter off at ballet class. Shouting through the open van window, he promises her that next time, he'll try to bring the vehicle to a complete stop as she's getting out. But there's no denying it was a TERRIFIC jump.

4:33 p.m.: Father races across town to drop son off at soccer practice.

"I'm gonna be late!" son says 43 times. Father responds: "Well, if you'd eaten your Rice Krispie square a little faster maybe we wouldn't be in this fix!" Son leaps from van to join fellow team members already on the field.

4:40 p.m.: Father drops into local donut shop for quick coffee and half a dozen crullers before heading back to pick up daughter when ballet class finishes.

Happens to notice part of large duffel bag through van window. Soccer gear.

4:45 p.m.: Father races back to soccer field, where son is standing by the road side, pacing. Son, upon grabbing bag, shouts: "Thanks a LOT!" He does not sound entirely sincere.

5:00 p.m.: Dad races back to the ballet school. Hears siren.

5:15 p.m.: Daughter wants to know why father is 15 minutes late. Says her MOTHER is never 15 minutes late, she always picks her up on time.

Father is too busy contemplating what three demerit points will do to his insurance rates to respond. Also wonders whether offering a police officer a cruller constitutes a bribe, or is just simply a stereotyping insult.

5:25 p.m.: Father, sweat streaming down his temples and neck and into his shirt, wheels into parking lot of local community center. "Have you got your bathing suit?" he asks.

Daughter rummages around in her ballet case. "Yup!" He takes her inside, where the humidity level from the pool makes it feel like the Amazon Basin. "Hurry, come on, your lesson starts in five minutes!" he says. Somewhat preoccupied, he follows her right into the ladies' change room, where he slips on a wet tile after glimpsing the president of the local home and school association stepping out of the shower.

Father offers profuse apologies, backs out of the change room with his eyes fixed to the floor, and races back to the van, where he is so full of remorse he immediately gets on the cell phone to ask his wife if she'd ever have believed that the woman in charge of volunteers for the school lunch-room program has a tattoo of Jerry Garcia on her thigh.

54

5:40 p.m.: Father momentarily forgets where his son is. Hockey practice? Boy Scouts? Tuba lessons? Self-tattooing classes? No, none of those. Of course! Soccer!

He makes a U-turn, forcing a busload of lawn bowlers into the ditch.

5:53 p.m.: Father returns to the soccer field and throws soccer equipment into back of van. The boy is covered in mud and grass stains, has blood trickling down from his nose, and smells as though someone has emptied the contents of a brewery over his head.

Father decides not to blow his stack, not to scream and yell, because it turns out this isn't his kid, it's somebody else's.

6:02 p.m.: With correct son now safely stowed in the back, father proceeds to deliver him to his next appointment, wrestling lessons, which are being held at an odd address out on the airport strip.

Once there, father discovers it is a place called Lola's, a noted adult entertainment parlor, and it's not wrestling, but MUD wrestling lessons. Even though there appears to have been some mistake made (father makes note to call producers of the parks and rec catalog to ask about this), son says, "What the hey, I think I'd like to take this anyway."

Father drags him out of the establishment, and snaps "never mind" when asked to explain how one of the dancers, Vanessa Vavoom, was able to smile and say hello to him, by name.

6:31 p.m.: Back at the community pool, father runs into reverse of problem he encountered at the soccer field: someone else has collected HIS daughter. But it turns out she was taken home in error by the McKinleys, who are not only good people, but also members of the Rotary Club, and should be able to give his daughter a good home.

6:46 p.m.: Father decides, upon reflection, that he better pick up his daughter at the McKinley house, especially since they will not be familiar with her various food allergies.

Once he has his own daughter back in the van, he wheels

through the McDonald's drive-through so he and the kids can all get something to eat before heading off to their last stop of the night, boys' and girls' pre-teen taxidermy lessons.

6:52 p.m.: Turns out they received, in error, two Big Macs, one Filet-O-Fish sandwich, fries, and three Cokes, instead of one Quarter Pounder with cheese, one regular hamburger, one pepperoni pizza, and milkshakes all around.

Father does another U-turn, sending into the ditch a busload of Norwegian mime artists on an international tour, and gets back in the drive-through line to complain about his order. But by the time he gets to the window to demand an exchange, his son has eaten everything, and needs to find a bathroom fast because he drank all the Cokes, too.

8:12 p.m.: They all arrive home from taxidermy class, where the kids learned some of the finer points about disguising moose mold. Father and kids give mom hugs, and the kids are instructed to get ready for bed and take one last look at their homework, just in case there's anything they need to have done for class tomorrow, as if anybody really cares.

9:30 p.m.: It's lights-out time for the kids. Father also falls into bed, swearing that he will never, EVER again be in charge of shuttling the kids from lesson to lesson to lesson and back home again.

4:15 a.m.: Son, decked out in hockey jersey, creeps quietly into parents' bedroom, where father is making chainsaw noises with his open mouth, and turns on the bedside table lamp.

"Dad? Dad? You didn't forget, did you? I gotta be at practice by five."

8

The Birthday Party

(Or: The Gucci Goodie Bag)

Please put out of your head all memories of the kind of birthday parties your parents threw for you when you were a child.

You know, the kind where you had four or five of your friends over, you played a little pin-the-tail-on-the-donkey, blew out candles, ate some cake, opened the presents, and then sent your friends home.

How passé. How totally '60s.

Shame on you, SHAME ON YOU, if this is the kind of birthday party you've thrown for a child of your own. Don't be surprised if a *60 Minutes* film crew led by Morley Safer bursts through your door any day now, exposing you as a parent who doesn't understand the meaning of the words "self-esteem," "positive self-image," and "line of credit."

The children of the new millennium will not sit still for a party that belongs to the days of Dennis the Menace.

If you are any kind of father at all, the first thing you must know is that any party worth its icing isn't even held at home, unless you have hired a clown, a magician, Fred Penner, the Barenaked Ladies, and the Harlem Globetrotters to perform in your backyard. (This list does not include, of course, the caterers.)

The really good parties are held outside the home. Possible sites include the local bowling alley, a sports club that offers such features as batting cages and basketball courts, the community pool, the local hockey arena, a fast-food joint, or Maple Leaf Gardens.

Some people think the demand for elaborate and far-from-home parties has grown because children are spoiled little brats who've come to expect this sort of thing because all their friends had parties like this, and only a geek would have a party IN HIS OWN HOME.

Well, this is all true, but the Number One reason parties are held outside the home is: broadloom.

Yes, it's actually parents who are behind this new trend in outlandish parties for infants. We are willing to fork out any amount of money to keep our kids' screaming, miserable, gum-chewing, chocolate-candy-bar-smeared, cake-coated, pop-drenched friends off our carpeting, even though we think nothing of having our own pâté-smeared, cigarette-smoking, alcohol-reeking adult friends over all the time.

Many parents will come to feel that, in the long run, they might have been better off just to get area rugs that could be rolled up when kids come over. Because now, every single year, we must find a new activity that's even better than that of the year before.

The Bowling Alley

If you're planning your child's very first party outside the home, the bowling alley is a good place to start. Most bowling alleys have special birthday deals: in addition to an hour of bowling, you get a party meal consisting of a hamburger, fries, and pop that would fail a health department inspection in even the most miserable Third World nation, but is considered acceptable if the business happens to be a bus terminal, theme park snack bar stand, or bowling alley.

For a dad, the bowling alley experience provides a wonderful opportunity to get to know your child's buddies in a friendly atmosphere of nonthreatening competition.

For example:

Your child: Hey, Donny, nice GUTTER ball!
Donny: Oh yeah? How'd you like this ball shoved down your throat, butthead!

Children become so excited waiting for their turn to throw the ball down the alley that it may become necessary for you to impose some small sense of order.

Dad: Courtney, don't stand in the other alley, sweethe— Michael! THAT way! The ball goes down the alley THAT way, not toward the pinball machi— Kristie, Kristie! Don't keep kicking the ball down there! It's not like soccer! Get back up — Adam! For the love of God it's not shot put! Hey, hey, nobody take a ball until it's their turn, there's no balls left! Who took my wallet? Hey, where are Billy and Franklin? Whaddya mean they've rented a pool table? And where — *(BOOONNNNKKKK!!!)* Milton, in bowling we do not throw overhand.

Bowling also offers you the chance to view scientific principles in a way you'd never dreamed — especially if you're taking very small children who like to slobber on the ball as much as they like to throw it.

For example: a body in motion does not always continue in motion.

Before taking a toddler bowling, you would never have thought it possible for a ball to stop halfway down the alley due to a lack of momentum. When this happens, you'll have to get an employee to gingerly walk down the alley and rescue the ball. (You can find him behind the snack bar, where, after he's retrieved the slobber-soaked ball, he will return to make your burgers.)

The Sleepover Party

If you are the kind of father who's already lost the will to live and is convinced that no matter what happens, things cannot get any worse, you might want to consider The Sleepover Party.

Decide first of all how many children you feel you can handle for an overnight stay at your home. If you say anything more than five, you really haven't thought this through.

Set aside a room where there's space to spread out several sleeping bags, and instruct parents to make sure their kids pack pajamas, a pillow, toothbrush, change of clothes for the morning, and a bottle of scotch for you. (They WILL do this, so go ahead and ask. When you are taking someone else's child off their hands for overnight, they will give you anything. If your child's best friend's parents own a Mazda dealership, ask for a Miata. Don't forget to specify color preference.)

Kids love to rent videos for sleepovers, particularly slasher movies, like the *Nightmare on Elm Street*, *Halloween*, and *Friday the 13th* series, where young teens get all sorts of bodily parts hacked off as punishment for French-kissing, feeling under each other's tops, and being stupid enough to walk in the basement of an old house where the lights don't work, calling out: "Heather? Are you down here, Heather?"

If your children are older than seven, however, you might want to try something more mature, like the Ernest movies (e.g., *Ernest Goes to Camp*, *Ernest Burps*, *Ernest Pees His Pants*, and the most cerebral of the series, *Ernest Farts*).

Don't worry about trying to get the kids to bed at a reasonable time. They'll want to talk all night, drink pop, eat chips, and tell ghost stories while holding a flashlight under their chin. Then, once they're finished, they'll all be so scared they'll demand to crawl into bed with you and your spouse. You had foolishly thought, what with having her friends over and all, that this would be the first night since March 1994 she wasn't in bed with you.

Although these kinds of parties can be quite a bit of work, at least you'll get to find out which of your child's playmates have incontinence problems.

Opening the Presents

Once the children have engaged in a few fun-filled activities and been force-fed enough snacks to lull them into a brief sugar stupor, it's time to open the gifts. Boys and girls perform this activity quite differently.

For example, when a present and accompanying card are handed

to a birthday girl, she will, having learned some good manners from her mother, actually *read the card.*

This will make the birthday girl's mother smile with pride, but drive her father, who is poised with camera and flash, totally nuts as he waits to record the moment when his daughter finally rips into the package to find her fourth Ice Pick Barbie. (This is the latest version of the popular dress-up doll, based on the Sharon Stone character in *Basic Instinct*. Includes one plastic ice pick; leather outfit and handcuffs are sold separately.)

Girls not only open the cards and read who they are from, but they will also read for all the assembled guests every treasured Hallmark word. Boys, on the other hand, can tear apart paper and box in a single move without noticing any card whatsoever. This makes their fathers very proud, since it means there hasn't been a lot of time wasted on unnecessary pleasantries.

The Thank-You Note

Oh, get a life.

The Goodie Bag

We don't know how the tradition of The Goodie Bag started. We have no memory of it from when we were kids. The whole idea of going to a birthday party was that YOU brought a present, got some cake and orange soda splattered across your new shirt and pants, and went home.

Somewhere along the line, during the Reagan years, it became customary for guests at a birthday party not only to arrive with gifts, but to leave with them as well. This, next to trying to undo knotted shoelaces, may be the single greatest aggravation suffered by parents in the tail end of this century.

All of this is complicated by the fact that YOU, not your child, will be judged by his friends' parents when they view the contents of The Goodie Bag. For example, this might be what you'd considered putting in The Goodie Bags for your own child's party:

- a small pack of Smarties
- a snap bracelet
- two pieces of gum

- three baseball cards
- small plastic car

Not bad, right? It's not THEIR birthday party, right? And you did give them cake, and took them to the bowling alley, and took them off THEIR parents' hands for a few hours.

All that would be fine, except this is what your child came home with in HER Goodie Bag when she attended the recent party of one of her friends:

- LARGE bag of Smarties
- four swirly suckers
- free passes to the opening night of the next Schwarzenegger movie, including dinner with the star
- keys to a Cabrio, held in trust until she turns 17
- tickets for a one-week, all-expenses-paid trip to Disney World
- 40 shares of Sprint Canada and lunch with Candice Bergen

Not only that, but it's come in one of those fancy bags from the Hallmark store, and you'd planned to put your kids' stuff in paper lunch bags with happy faces drawn on the side with magic marker.

You have to decide now whether you want to go into debt, or make a point with your child that it's not how much one spends on a birthday party, but the thought and the love behind it, and then, when your child grows up, see his book, *Cheated Out of Birthday Bliss: One Victim's Story*, rise to the top of the bestseller charts.

Hey, the choice is yours.

9

Making Your Kids Proud of You

(Or: 25 simple steps to appearing god-like to children who wouldn't know Zeus if he came over and recharged the batteries for their Game Boys)

As silly (and pitiful) as it may seem, dads really love to show off for their own kids.

Nothing fills a dad with more pride than to see his children look at him adoringly, with absolute wonder and worship in their eyes.

"Good gosh!" those eyes seem to be saying. "This man is more than just our Dad. He is the most astonishing, strongest, smartest, most heroic man on the face of the planet."

Children hold this high opinion of their fathers mainly because they have formed it in the absence of all the facts. They are operating on limited information.

This is why fathers love their children so much. Kids, especially the younger ones, are still pretty dumb — dumb enough, at least, to consider their dads as somewhat god-like.

But mothers, who have been on the scene much longer, know that if their husbands did, in fact, have the power and wisdom of gods, they would be much better at remembering where things go when they unload the dishwasher, and might — just MIGHT — finally get around to fixing the toilet upstairs, which has been trickling since before the final episode of *M*A*S*H*. When, for example, was the last time you heard Zeus say: "Geez, honey, why don't you just jiggle the handle?"

The same can be said for the people many fathers work with.

They are, beyond a doubt, unlikely to confuse his performance with that of a god's, unless you are talking about the kind of damage that can be caused by so-called "acts of God," like hurricanes and floods. (Although, to be fair, the father's coworkers may often use the Lord's name to describe him or his performance in the workplace, as in: "God love a duck, but if that ain't the most inventive excuse I ever did hear for not meeting your sales target: Being secretly recruited by the CIA to assassinate a Latin American dictator.")

But with children, it's a different story.

All they know is that this is their daddy, the one who hugs them, the one who plays with them, the one who somehow just HAS to find his tire pressure gauge, even though he owns neither a car nor a bike, whenever a diaper needs changing.

Fathers like to establish a certain kind of image for their kids. They want to appear powerful, ever youthful. They want to give the impression that the years have not passed them by, that they are still up on the latest trends. They want to appear wise and all-knowing.

Sometimes this involves lying.

But you figure, if it's for a good cause, like making kids feel their fathers are extra special, then what exactly is the harm?

25 Things You Can Do

Here are 25 sure-fire, no-fail, confidence-building, image-enhancing ways to impress your sons and daughters. Use them at your own risk.

1. From here on, drop your name and be known only by a symbol. The kids can refer to you as "The Parental Unit Formerly Known As Dad." (Choose the international dad symbol, the wallet.)

2. Just because you're into your 30s or 40s doesn't mean you can't get in there and play sports with the young ones. When you find the kids getting into a good game of driveway basketball, jump in, grab the ball, shoot a few baskets, and run yourself ragged.

3. Once you've proven you still have what it takes to dazzle them on the basketball court, give everyone some high fives, go inside, and find a nice, private place, where your kids will not be able to observe you, to roll up into a ball and die.

4. Every time you drive by a cemetery, say to the kids in the backseat: "People are just dyin' to get in there!" Dads have been using this for decades, and it's a guaranteed knee-slapper.

5. When it's Career Day at your kids' school, volunteer to go in.

   Your children, who are DEEPLY and GENUINELY concerned about the incredibly busy schedule you keep as a parking lot attendant, will try to dissuade you.

   "Gee, Dad, we wouldn't want you to go to all that trouble of bringing your BOOTH in."

   It may be necessary for you to call the school directly to offer your services. But it will be worth the trouble, when you're able to stand up there in front of an entire class, and your own kids, and see them beaming with pride as you recite the parking lot attendant's credo: "No in-and-out privileges. And I don't have change for a fifty."

6. Tell them that when you were younger, you were in the war, and killed a man. If they ask WHICH war, say it was a "price war," and that you zapped the guy with a bar code reader.

7. Show them that you are committed to the environment and conservation by walking around the house and shouting: "Who left all these lights on?"

8. Tell them that sure, through the DAY you sell carpeting, but at NIGHT, after they've gone to bed, you don your crime fighting costume and track down disreputable salesmen passing off plain old rugs as Stainmaster-protected. You are Fiberman.

9. Show them you can break windows with your belches. (Don't demonstrate this when their mother is home.)

10. Tell them you used to hang out on the beach where they film *Baywatch*. Tell them you know Pamela Whatserface personally.

11. Without in any way suggesting that you could have done better (because you know, in your heart, that with your wife you've done better than you ever deserved to), tell your kids you were QUITE the catch as a young man before you met their mother. You were handsome and dashing and sophisticated and all the girls were after you.

   To prove the point,[1] dig out an old picture of yourself. Explain to your children, who are now clutching their sides in pain from the laughter, that it was considered suave and debonair at that time to look like a member of the Brady Bunch.

12. Demonstrate for the children that the days when fathers knew how to fix things around the house are, despite what they might have heard from their mother, hardly over. Show them that with a few simple tools — measuring tape, screw driver, hammer, cement mixer — and a mere seven days, you can hang a blind.

13. When the kids ask you to go Rollerblading with them, say: "You betcha!"

14. Demonstrate your toughness by not crying, even though your spleen has just been ruptured by a 1993 Corolla, which you slid under after leaving the sidewalk following the shortest recorded Rollerblade ride in history: 4.3 seconds.

---

[1] As if you needed to.

15. Show the kids that, while it's important SOMETIMES to be tough, there's no shame in crying when the ambulance attendants, who are falling over, guffawing because this is the third Rollerblading-dad-gets-ruptured-spleen incident they've had since coming on shift, accidentally drop you into the path of a streetcar.

16. When the kids get scared about a little spider in the bedroom, go in there and snare it in a tissue, and joke about how even when an itsy-bitsy spider bites you, as this one just did, it doesn't hurt one little bit.

17. Later, when you are starting to feel slightly funny (defined as losing the ability to see and breathe), demonstrate your interest in science and nature by calling the local bug expert to ask if this isn't an odd part of the country to encounter a black widow spider.

18. Grab your child's nose, then pull your hand away, tucking your thumb between your first two fingers and say: "Got your nose!" (Note: Kids get a bit weary of this around the time they're 18.)

19. When you rent *2001: A Space Odyssey* to show the kids that they were making pretty terrific science fiction movies long before the *Star Wars* saga, impress the socks off them, when they appear to be totally baffled, by explaining what the Stanley Kubrick masterpiece REALLY means.

   "Man's knowledge, his quest to explore and evolve," you say, "all came from touching a massive, black, 2 by 4."

20. Make your ears wiggle.

   (If you're unable to do this, try wiggling your nostrils rabbit-like. If you can't do that, do that trick where you put your hands together, then pull them apart to make it look like you've disconnected your index finger. And if you can't even do THAT, well, you should reconsider fatherhood altogether.)

21. Tell the kids you know how they got the caramel into the Caramilk bars from your days working with the Secret Service.

22. Ask them if they remember that historic moment in sports in 1993 when Joe Carter went leaping around the bases after hitting that homer at the SkyDome and clinching the World Series for a second time for the Blue Jays. Well, you went to school with Joe Carter, although it was not the SAME Joe Carter. This was the Joe Carter, dryer repairman.
23. To prove to the kids that you could just as easily have been a major entertainer as a manufacturer of dental floss, do your version of *Sunset Boulevard* using finger puppets.
24. Show your kids what a terrific, photographic memory you have. For example: "Okay Brian, Melinda, I want you to arrange a dozen of your toys in front of me in any order you want, then I will turn my back and tell you, EXACTLY, what order they were in."

    "I'm *Melissa*, Dad."

    "Uh, Dad, it's Bryant, not Brian."
25. Get them to pull your finger.

What Real People Say and Do

Of course, what makes your children most proud of you can depend very much on who you are and what line of work you're in.

For example, if you are an enforcer for the local mob, coming home at the end of the day and telling your kids you busted three knees and hung a guy out a 20-storey window will make them positively beam.

However, if you're the CEO of a major corporation, coming home with the same news is going to be a real letdown, because you're supposed to have people who can do that sort of thing for you.

But if you can report that you've crushed three opposing companies right out of existence, throwing hundreds out of work and doubling your profits at the same time, well, prepare yourself to be adored. This is definitely a day to celebrate.

Here are a few examples of professions and real people, who may or may not yet be fathers, and the kinds of words of wisdom young people can expect to hear from them.

Major league baseball player: "The important thing to remember is, getting to play in the majors is a great gift, the kind of thing most people only dream about, and you must never forget that, provided the bastards give you your $5 million a year."

Michael Jackson (singer, friend of children): "It don't matter if you're black or white, or male or female, because you can always get it fixed."

Member of Canada's Senate: "If there's one thing you better learn in this life, son, it's the importance of an afternoon nap."

Member of the U.S. Senate: "Let me give you just ONE word of advice: Happy hour."

Prince Charles (monarchy guy): "I know your little head must hurt just AWFULLY, having fallen off the top of the slide when those beastly little common children tossed you off, and I'd love to stay with you here in the hospital, but there's a lovely play opening tonight and I fear it would embarrass you terribly if I weren't there."

Prince Andrew (monarchy guy's brother): "Oh for the love of Pete, this is the absolute last time I'm going to read you one of these wretched Budgie the Helicopter stories."

Fabio (model and winner of the Nobel Prize for Hair): "Duh."

10

The School Trip

(Or: "Dad, what are you doing behind that tree?")

Back in the days when they still built houses with those little doors in the side for milk delivery, when the word "hurl" only meant "to throw" instead of "throw up," if your child's school needed a parent volunteer, they always called on the mother to help out.

Back then, the mother was always home. It was ASSUMED that she'd be home, as it was equally assumed that dad would not be, unless he was some useless layabout, sitting around watching TV and scratching himself in particularly hard-to-reach places.

School officials did not expect, when calling on mom to help out with a school activity, that she would have to put a real-estate deal on hold or tell her client that, hey, she couldn't defend him today against charges of fraud and embezzlement because she had to help make gingerbread houses in her son's Grade 3 class.

Nowadays mothers are employed outside the home nearly as much as fathers, and schools are finding themselves in a real pickle when it comes to finding extra help for an outing.

This is where the sensitive '90s dad comes in.

He understands that bonding with his kids, being a part of their school experience, and getting to know their teachers are every bit as important as balancing the company's books, making that extra sale, or looking for tax loopholes on behalf of filthy rich clients, unless of course this is the date of the firm's annual golf day, in which case there must be SOME other parent who hasn't got a life who could go spend a day with a bunch of whining, runny-nosed students.

But seriously, most fathers are glad to take a day away from the office to help with a class trip, if only because the next time a trip comes up, they can say to their wives: "Hey, I went last time, on the zoo trip, and I still haven't been able to get that platypus poo out of the treads of my Florsheims, so it's your turn."

These school trips can actually be a lot of fun. At least, this is what the teachers will tell you. You may get a free trip to the science center, or the planetarium, or maybe even the museum, where you'll be able to see all kinds of interesting things, including dinosaurs, Indian relics, and your daughter sneaking behind the velvet rope to crawl into a sarcophagus.

But as luck will have it, on THIS particular day, you're accompanying your child on a Wilderness Discovery Adventure.

This will see you boarding a bus with two teachers, two other parent volunteers, and 379 children on Ritalin IV drips, for a four-hour ride. Once you are clear of the city limits, the teachers will herd everyone off the bus to examine a chunk of moss, then get you and the students back on the bus for the trip home.

Even though this is the '90s, the two other parent volunteers will be women, and they will sit together on the bus, every once in a while glancing your way.

They will be talking about you. The conversation will go something like this:

Mother #1: What do you suppose he's doing here?

Mother #2: I think he must be out of work. I mean, LOOK at how his daughter's dressed. NOTHING from The Gap.

Mother #1: You must be right. Unless this is how he gets his kicks, hanging out with little children.

Mother #2: Oh my God, Mildred, you might be on to something there. Look, look at how he watches the kids. You can almost guess what he's thinking. I'm going to mention something to the principal when we get back.

Mother #1: Doesn't he look like that pervert who was on *America's Most Wanted* the other night?

Mother #2: A dead ringer. Next time we stop I'll get to a pay phone and call the police.

But if you're any kind of decent father, you're not going to let some idle gossip or what other people think deter you.

What really matters is you're getting a chance to spend some real quality time with your child.

She will be quick to show her gratitude.

"Dad, do you have to sit WITH me on the bus? Couldn't you sit with one of the moms or Mrs. Cowlick? I want to sit with Jamie. You're *embarrassing* me."

This is the same child who made a special construction paper card that said "You are the BEST Dad in the world" just so you'd come along, and then wept uncontrollably when you suggested, only for a moment, that you might not be able to get the day off.

So you switch seats and end up sitting with a little boy named Ronald, who so far hasn't been able to get anyone to sit with him because he's, well, a little bit DIFFERENT, some might even say DISTURBED, but you view this as a chance to show the other children that just because a youngster doesn't immediately fit in, that's no reason to shun him.

He warms up to you right away, and asks: "Have you ever cut open a live squirrel? Would you like to see the one I just did?"

Getting the Day Off

We've seen some tremendous changes in attitudes among employers. It started back in the '80s, and has continued on through the '90s.

Corporations are beginning to understand that if a worker's home life is secure and happy, they're going to have a more productive employee. That's why companies now bend over backwards to accommodate a worker's family needs. And that now includes men, too.

For example:

Male employee: So, uh, listen, I was wondering if I could come in a bit late Thursday so I could go help my kid at school. They're doing a lesson on apples and I'm to help them make applesauce.
Boss: Don't you have a wife?

Depending on your boss's personality, you may want to adopt a different strategy. Sometimes a better plan is not to ask for the time off in advance, but to show up late on that Thursday morning.

When the boss hauls you into his office, make up a good story.

Boss: Where the hell have you been? I've been covering for you all morning.
Employee: Gosh, I'm sorry, but I went to this place for a drink after work with Sheila, you know, the woman down in accounting, the one with the big, well, you know . . .
Boss: Yeah? Sure, sure, I know. You and Sheila?
Employee: Yeah, so we got to having a few drinks, and well, before you know it I was calling home to say I had to work a bit late, and one thing led to another, and the alarm didn't go off —
Boss: Why, Smithers, you ol' son of a gun, out sharpening the old pencil, were ya? Listen, take the rest of the day off, you look terrible!

This way your true shame, of taking time off to spend with your kid, remains a secret.

The following chart sets out various employee indiscretions and how enlightened companies tend to deal with them. The business world is a lot more understanding these days than most people realize.

How most companies handle various situations

Drunk at work.	Company sends you at its expense for four weeks to lavish resort to dry out.
Skip work to attend afternoon major league baseball game.	Through an incredible fluke, your seats are right next to the boss, who is so thrilled that you have a common interest, he promotes you.
Steal office computers and resell them on the underground market for 10 percent more than the going rate.	Your company finds out, but is so impressed by what a great wheeler-dealer you are that they put you in charge of the retail division.
Take morning off to bond with your child on school trip.	Fired.

What You'll Need for the School Trip

Don't forget, if you have to pack a lunch for your child, you'll need one, too. But you don't have to settle for a peanut butter sandwich and a Twinkie. Pack yourself a sleeve of water crackers, some fine cheeses, and a small container of goose liver pâté. This last should be held in reserve as an excellent disciplinary tool. When dealing with a disruptive child, show him the pâté and threaten to make him eat some if he doesn't settle down.

Here are a few other things you may want to bring.

- Extra Strength Tylenol (caplets, as they are easier to swallow without water)
- industrial earplugs
- duct tape (one roll for every 10 children)
- disguise (in case your child turns out to be the worst behaved, you can disavow any responsibility)
- disguise for child (in case you turn out to be a terrible embarrassment to her)
- cell phone and portable fax machine for keeping in touch with the office
- *Wall Street Journal*
- Walkman
- lion tamer's stool and whip
- Band-Aids
- hip flask

A Last-Minute Tip

Whatever kind of trip you're going on, if it's going to involve some time on a bus, skip your morning coffee.

If it's been a long time since you were on a school bus, you may have forgotten that they do not have washrooms. These are not Greyhound luxury cruisers.

The absence of facilities certainly increases the likelihood that some small children may have an unfortunate accident while en route to your destination, but at least they will be forgiven.

If you are to have a similar accident, it is unlikely to be glossed over quite so quickly, particularly not by the two mothers who saw you on *America's Most Wanted*.

The truth is, most children can hold it for longer than adults. If you take a look at the adult volunteers on the school bus, they're the ones with their legs tightly crossed.

You must keep all this in mind, even if you are going on a wilderness trip.

Just because you're in the middle of the woods, it's not safe to duck behind a tree to take a quick whiz. Some child will always spot you, then tell all the others. Once the other children get back home, they will tell their parents: "Mr. Whipple took out his thing in the woods. It was so GROSS!"

This can lead to a decline in one's standing in the community and odd stares at parent–teacher night, although it pretty much clinches it that you'll never be asked to go on one of these trips again.

11

The Car Trip

(Or: "Stop looking out my window, pus-head!")

There is nothing quite like the motor trip to bring a family closer together.

For 50 weeks of the year you all head your separate ways each morning, never able to share some real TIME together, but on a car trip the miracle of the combustion engine and a network of the most fantastic highways on the planet mean that mom and dad and the kids can head out together on an incredible adventure, seeking out new horizons, trading stories, playing games, singing songs, counting blue cars, then green cars, then Hondas, then Fords, then cars with out-of-province license plates, then cars with one headlight out, then any old miserable clunker, then roadkill, then barnyard animals attempting to mount one another in plain view at the side of the road, ANYTHING to help pass the time, to keep the kids from asking "Are we there yet?" as the minutes, then the hours, drag by, mile after brutally agonizing mile.

Yes, the motor trip is a terrific experience that every family should do at least once, and the key to making it a success is bringing along lots of activities to keep the kids from getting bored.

Some of these things include Walkmans, small puzzles, card games, books, and plenty of paper and crayons, which, if left in a locked car on a summer's day for any more than three minutes, will melt right into the upholstery of your new Buick Park Avenue.

If you're smart enough to plan ahead and fill a case with all these activities for your youngster, you can be assured that he'll remain entertained roughly until you've backed the car down to the end of your driveway.

After that point, you will be regaled with the never-ending refrain: "I'm bored. I don't have anything to do. I have a headache."

Not to mention the ever-popular: "I have to go to the bathroom."

Children's bladders, which seem to be able to go several days without emptying under normal circumstances, are particularly sensitive on trips along interstate highways, where you can sometimes travel halfway across the continental United States without ever passing an exit or rest stop.

"Okay, everybody, there's a service center one mile ahead, and the next one isn't for 976 miles. Does anyone have to go to the bathroom NOW or can you wait for the next one?"

"I don't have to go!"

"Me neither!"

"You sure?"

Together: "We're sure! We're fine! Just keep going! We want to GET there!"

Approximately 1/767th of a mile after you pass the service center, a small voice from the backseat will say: "I have to go."

"OH FOR THE LOVE OF GOD!" says you, the understanding, patient, loving father. "I'll pull over to the side of the road, for heaven's sake."

"But it's *(big dramatic pause)* Number Two."

79

No other announcement, except for perhaps your wife mentioning that all the traveler's checks are missing, can grip a car full of vacationing family members with complete panic as quickly. A sense of foreboding, of imminent doom, pervades. Sometimes siblings can be very helpful at times like these, providing regular updates on the condition of the child who desperately needs to find a washroom.

"Oh God, Dad, I think he's gonna blow."

The Slammed-Car-Door Problem

One thing you will want to have a talk with your children about is how to close the rear doors. This is important every day of the year, but especially so when you are on a car trip far from home.

Once children get past the age of six, and develop a bit of strength in their upper arms, they REALLY want to be sure that when they close that back door, it's absolutely, positively, without a doubt CLOSED.

To achieve this, they will swing the door closed so incredibly hard that if Toronto Blue Jays pitcher Juan Guzman used this kind of force, his rotator cup would fly right out of the SkyDome and smash someone's windshield on the Gardiner Expressway.

Few people are aware that one of the biggest worries among car manufacturers, in Detroit and in Japan, is that no vehicle has been built that will withstand, over lengthy periods of time, the "slamming tests" at automotive proving grounds.

Researchers found that the heads of crash test dummies that had earlier survived 100-mile-per-hour front-end collisions, when subjected to a rear door slammed shut by an 11-year-old eager to catch up with his friends heading into school, exploded.

Fragments of skull were scattered all over the place, but not before the dummy shouted out: "Hey, make sure you don't slam the —"

BOOOOMMMM!!!

Similar incidents, involving real people, have been documented across Canada and the United States. For example, the following statement, taken from a nine-year-old girl, is from an actual police report filed in Vulcan, Alberta.

"So like, I got, like, out of the car and, like, I started to close the door, and, like, my Dad started shouting something, and then, like, there was this big, like, EXPLOSION, in the car, and, like, I don't know what I'm going to do, because, like, someone has to take me to ballet practice after school."

No amount of asking children to close the doors with a little less force seems to work. They remain convinced that if they do not slam the door, it will not latch completely, thereby leaving the interior dome light on all day and all night. Then, the next morning, the car's battery will be dead and the car will not start.

The kids do not want this. If the car can't start, they can't sleep in and count on one of their parents to drive them to school in a complete panic at the last minute. If they KNOW the car won't work, they'll be forced to get up on time and actually WALK to school, which they absolutely do NOT want, because they might actually have to carry a book or something.

Now, all of this is particularly important when you are on vacation, especially if you are driving through one of those terrific tourist attractions, the wilderness safari.

This is the kind of park where you can actually see, from the safety of your enclosed, air-conditioned automobile, such wild animals as baboons, lions, elephants, and tigers running completely free. This is one of the best places to observe a beautiful beast of the jungle, in its natural habitat, rip the windshield wipers off your car and pee all over your hood.

So, when you have just entered the grounds of a wilderness park, and your child hops out to pet an anteater, and you call out to him: "GETINTHECAR! GETINTHECAR! GETINTHECAR!!!!!" you can expect that when he returns he's going to give that door a pretty solid "WHACK!"

At this point the window will disintegrate into nine million little pieces, not only covering the interior with glass shards, but also allowing some of nature's most intestinally carefree creatures to hop inside and leave you a souvenir, or, if they are so inclined, eat you.

Territorial Disputes

Occasionally (as in, all the time), if you have more than one child, disputes over territory will erupt in the backseat of the car.

Sometimes they will be over seemingly trivial things, like when one child, trying to stretch out for a nap, sticks his not-been-washed-for-2,876-miles feet in his sister's face.

But other times they will be over serious issues, as in: "Stop looking out my window! That's MY window and if I catch you looking out it again I'll kill you!"

Something auto manufacturers have overlooked is a rear seat that has a clearly marked dividing line. Often, the patterns and weaves in car upholstery leave in doubt where, exactly, the line of death (should a sibling dare cross it) is located.

One thing worth considering is a Plexiglas divider, much like the ones that cab drivers use to keep their backseat customers from killing them. But this divider is mounted in the opposite direction, cutting the backseat in two.

Your children will still be able to see each other, even press their lips to the glass and make extremely disgusting expressions of derision, but they'll be unable to touch each other or have any of their entertainment items move across the center line.

If your kids are especially unruly, and you're willing to spend a little bit extra, you can upgrade and get the *bulletproof* glass. (See your dealer for full details.)

It's worth noting here that disciplining your children while traveling can depend a lot on whether you drive Japanese or North American cars.

While cars made on this continent tend to be a little larger on average, that also means it requires a longer reach to grab at kids sitting in the backseat. If you wish to reach into the back to grab one of your youngins by the scruff of the neck, and you don't have long arms to begin with, you might want to consider something smaller like a Honda Civic, as opposed to a Ford Taurus.

(We know of one father who, years ago, got around this problem completely by keeping at his side on the front seat a fly swatter. When the kids gave him a hard time, he grabbed the swatter and shouted: "Take that! And that!" Of course, even to suggest such a method of disciplining a child in this day and age would be perilous. Police are everywhere watching for drivers who fail to keep both hands on the wheel.)

You are mistaken if you think the kinds of problems that stem from packing kids together like sardines can be solved by purchasing a minivan. This, in fact, only exacerbates things. Instead of a fight over one seat, the children are now strangling each other over access to two rows of seating.

"I want the BACKseat!"

"I got here first, you get the MIDDLE seat!"

"It's MY TURN to have the backseat! You had the backseat all the way from Albany!"

"You have a stupid face!"

"Do not!"

"Do so!"

"YOU KIDS STOP FIGHTING OVER THE SEATS THIS INSTANT! JUDY, YOU'VE HAD THE BACKSEAT FOR AGES! MURRAY, IT'S YOUR TURN TO TAKE THE BACK! NOW MOVE IT AND STOP ALL THIS FIGHTING!!!!"

There is, briefly, some quiet in the back of the van while the seat exchange is conducted.

Then:

"I wanted the middle seat anyway. Now I've got the headphone jacks."

"You can't use those, I'm putting MY headphones in there."

"You're not ALLOWED. Only the middle person can use the headphone jacks. It says so right in the manual."

"It does not."

"Does so."

"I've decided I don't want to sit in the back. You can have your stupid backseat back. I'm sitting in the middle."

"No you're not, you big pus-filled stink face."

"DAAAAAADDDDDYYYYY!!!!"

This brings us to our next, most obvious topic.

The Bridge Abutment

If you're the kind of father who thinks the only logical solution to ending problems of this nature is to drive your vehicle at top speed into the nearest bridge abutment, there's something very important that you should know.

Most vehicles today are equipped with air bags, and there's a very good chance that you're going to survive. And if you do, things are going to be WORSE for you than they were before, because the people at your insurance company are going to be very, VERY disappointed in you.

They are going to punish you for being so careless as to survive what years ago would have been a surefire way to make traveling a much quieter experience (not counting, of course, the noise that occurs on impact).

They are going to jack up your premiums so high that you may be forced to abandon owning a vehicle completely, meaning that the next time you decide to take a vacation, you will have to go by bus.

You might not think it possible, but this is even more horrendous than taking a family trip in your own vehicle, because if your kids persist in asking the Greyhound driver, "Are we there yet?" he will drop you ALL off at the nearest Wendy's, which may be a lovely fast-food enterprise and all, but is not exactly the kind of place where you'd like to spend the only two weeks you have off all year.

12

Going on Vacation

(Or: The Elevator Button Wars)

In the previous chapter, we discussed the fun of motor trips.

But what if your vacation is more destination-oriented? Perhaps you've booked a week away someplace, at a lodge, on a cruise ship, at a campsite, or at Walt Disney World.

If so, there are plenty of other things to keep in mind.

The Camping Trip

The camping trip is very popular among parents who don't know any better.

Many fathers have the romantic notion that pitching a tent in the wilderness (which is not REALLY the wilderness, but a provincial camping ground where 43,000 other people are also getting away from it all by playing Guns N' Roses full tilt on their ghetto blasters), sleeping on the ground with your kids, battling mosquitoes the size of Micro Machines, cooking wieners and beans for breakfast, lunch, and dinner, lining up with total strangers to brush your teeth and take a shower in a public washroom facility that's in such a state that if it were in a Third World country it would prompt the United Nations to intervene, and battling deranged raccoons (Nature's safecrackers) who have figured out how to get into your cooler and drink all your beer, is fun.

They are mistaken. It is not.

But kids love camping excursions because they provide an outdoors experience unlike anything they can get in the city or the suburbs. For example, where else but in the woods can kids see poison ivy for the first time, learn that grizzlies like salt and vinegar chips as much as berries, and find little forest creatures like grubs and spiders right in their very own sleeping bags?

So if you're still convinced that you want to do this, here's an important piece of advice you should remember: when it's pouring buckets of rain in the middle of the night, and you desperately feel the need to make a trip to the washroom, note that tent doors usually allow you to open the zipper just an inch at a height that is convenient for you. This should do perfectly.

Just be fast so that one of those cute forest creatures, like the furry-tailed Bobbitt, does not come along and bite you.

Staying in a Hotel

Children absolutely love hotels. And we're not talking here of The Plaza in Manhattan. We are talking any kind of hotel, including those ones along the side of interprovincial and interstate highways.

While you may be looking for certain things when YOU check into a hotel (price, cleanliness, proximity to various tourist attractions, a complimentary breakfast, a bar), your children will be judging it from a totally different perspective. For instance, does the room have one of those armoire/wardrobe things they can lock each other in?

These are the main things they are looking for when it comes to accommodation:

1. Are the beds good for bouncing? The last thing they want is some bed-and-breakfast kind of place with antique four-posters that collapse after one good vault.
2. Are there pop, ice, and candy bar machines on the same floor as the room?
3. Is your room at the end of a long hallway they can race down?
4. Is the room, at the very least, on the second floor? Any half decent stay at a hotel includes elevator travel.
5. Is there Pay-TV?

Now, let's take a look at some of these requirements in detail.

Beds

Hotel room beds, at least in the major chains, are incredibly durable things. If you peer under them, chances are you'd find a cement foundation. (This would be a great idea to take back home with you, eliminating the need to vacuum underneath, which, if you are like most guys, is something you occasionally forget for several decades at a time.) You could plunk a drowsy elephant on one of these suckers and it wouldn't sag an inch.

But the mattresses still have a good spring to them, and are the next best things to trampolines as far as your kids are concerned. They know *instinctively* that these beds are, in only an incidental kind of way, used for sleeping. Their real function, their primary purpose, is to assist them in banging their heads into the ceiling.

And they love to imagine that the couple of feet between the beds is the Grand Canyon, and so your children LEAP across the crevasse! Back and forth, again and again! Shrieking and laughing, slipping off the edge, banging into the end tables, knocking lamps onto the floor.

And you know what? Who cares? It's not YOUR place, right? And if the hotel people don't have the smarts to make beds strong enough to support 23-year-old twins having a little bit of fun, well, it just serves them right.

Vending Machines

Is it any wonder that your kids want a room near the vending machines?

This is the ultimate kid fantasy: to have just outside your bedroom door a seemingly endless supply of stuff that's bad for you.

If you're booking into a hotel right next to Niagara Falls, and the kids are given a choice between a room that looks directly over this wonder of nature, or a room just a few steps from the machines that dispense ice, Orange Crush, Mars bars, and Lay's Potato Chips, well, if you DON'T KNOW which one they'll pick, then it's time you introduced yourself to them.

The Long Hallway

Once the elevator reaches your floor, and the door opens, your children will explode from it like Olympic sprinters when the starter's pistol goes off. This will be a race to the death, legs and arms pumping. This can actually be a good thing, since it helps kids burn off some excess energy,[1] provided none of the following things happens.

1. Another guest emerges from a room.
2. Someone (guest or employee) emerges from a room carrying a room service tray.
3. Your children are wearing flip-flop sandals. (A boy or girl running full tilt in flip-flops can cause an accident similar to what happens when one car smashes into another at the start of the Indianapolis 500.)

We are talking complete and total annihilation. One second your child is running, the next you're down at the front desk, asking if you can get an extra pillow and a neck brace.

Even a child without siblings will race down the hall ahead of

---

[1] Oh yeah, don't you wish.

you, although to what purpose is not clear. The child SEEMS to think that if he gets there first, he will be able to get into the room before you, even though he does not have the key. Upon arriving at the door and realizing this, he will look at you impatiently, jump up and down, and, if you're having a really good day, wet his pants.

Elevators

There is nothing children enjoy fighting over more than who gets to press the elevator buttons. As a concerned father, you must ward off potential problems by deciding ahead of time who will get to press what. Take the case of the following father, who is explaining the rules for his children, Russell and Maggie.

Daddy: Now listen up, guys. When we get to the elevator, Russell, you may press the down button. And when we get INSIDE the elevator, you, Maggie, may press the button for the first floor. Russell, do you understand? The down button?

Russell: I understand.

Daddy: And Maggie, you press the button INSIDE the elevator. Understand?

Maggie: I understand.

Daddy: Okay, sign here. *(Presents documents to both children.)* And again, on the next page, press hard so it goes through to the carbons.

But, three steps away from the elevator, Maggie loses all control and bolts forward, jabbing at the down button OUTSIDE the elevator as though possessed.

Russell, who has seen this coming and has stopped at the ice machine along the way, slips a cube down the back of his sister's blouse and holds it there while she screams.

You grab hold of both of them, shaking them in a manner that would, perhaps, suggest to a stranger that you have completely and totally lost your mind, at which point the elevator will open and a hotel security officer will step out, throw you up against the wall so that you can taste the wallpaper, kick your feet apart, and bark into his radio that he needs backup on the third floor. Meanwhile, your children will dash into the elevator, press ALL the buttons, and have the most fun they've had all week.

Pay-TV
The first thing your children will look for when you check into a new hotel room is the pamphlet on top of the television that tells what movies can be ordered and when, and for how much.

"Dad, Dad, DAAAADDD! This is AWESOME! We can get *Body of Perversion*, the one with Madonna, right here on the TV! Can we order it, huh, can we, CAN WE?"

"No."

"UhhHHHHHHH! Why not? Oh! OH! At 9:30 tonight we can get *Kung Fu Liver Kickers*! Whaddya say? Can we get that? Or at 8 we can watch *Alien 4: Chestbursters on Parade*! It's only $4.95 added to the bill! Awwww, DAAADDDDD!"

"No."

Grab this program from your kids and slip it into a drawer where they won't find it again for the duration of your stay. But first, point out to your wife the naughty number they're running at midnight, and IF the kids are asleep . . .

No, forget it. You can just absolutely, positively FORGET IT, as we'll explain in our next section.

Sleeping Arrangements

Children love vacations for so many reasons. The change in routine, getting to see new things, the endless opportunities to hound their parents for souvenirs and gifts, and the chance to sleep in the same bed with mom and dad.

91

Take the typical family of four as they walk into a hotel room with two double beds in it.

"I want to sleep with Mom!"

"I want to sleep with Dad!"

There is no point in fighting this. Trying to sleep with one of your kids thrashing about in bed with you may sound horrendous, but the alternative is even worse.

Putting two young siblings, who normally do not sleep together, into the same bed is akin to locking two rabid pit bull terriers together in a closet. They won't settle down until one of them is dead.

"Stop hogging the covers!"

"You poked me in the back!"

"I did not! I did NOT poke her!"

"He just poked me! Right when he said he wasn't poking me, he was poking me in the back!"

"STOP POKING YOUR SISTER IN THE BACK!!!!"

"But she's been hogging all the covers!"

"STOP HOGGING ALL YOUR BROTHER'S COVERS!!!!"

"Poke alert! Poke alert!"

The only thing left to do is split them up in the hopes that they'll finally fall asleep.

But the only problem now is, it's only 9:12 p.m.

You and your spouse are not the least bit interested in going to sleep, but must not breathe, talk, watch television, or flip the pages of a magazine, for fear of preventing the children from drifting off.

So, finally, dying for a little conversation, both of you go into the bathroom and close the door, where you sit on the edge of the tub and your wife sits on the toilet with the seat down. And you tell yourself $2,500 was a small price to pay for a vacation where you get to share some really special time with your mate in such splendiferous surroundings, which just happen to include some lovely complimentary guest soaps.

Finding a Bathroom

Unless you're visiting a tourist attraction that's geared exclusively to kids, you must always be thinking about places to go to the bathroom.

Just as you should be conscious of where your wallet is when you're in a bad part of town, walking through the airport, or at home when your kids say they need pizza money, you must always be on the lookout for places to take your kids when they suddenly announce that the dam is about to burst.

Nobody out there wants to let you use their bathroom. That is because (and if you don't believe this just stop anywhere along a U.S. interstate highway) most tourists behave in a manner very similar to barnyard animals, except that the barnyard animals don't usually knock the hot-air dryers off the wall.

This is one of the few times when you will actually recall with fondness the days when your children were in diapers. Back then, they could go wherever and whenever they wanted.

But once children get into their early teens it's hard to get them to strap on a Huggies, so your bathroom radar must always be in high gear. This may mean forcing your children to go to the bathroom, even when they protest that they do not need to, for the simple reason that you've FOUND ONE.

"But I'm telling you, Dad, I don't have to go!"

"Then drink this, and THEN go!"

Value for the Dollar

Keep in mind: The more you spend on a holiday, the more your child will become overwhelmed and be unable to remember any of it.

After you've returned from a $6,000 Walt Disney World holiday where your children rode Space Mountain, got Mickey's autograph, and snuck in the back way to short-circuit Abraham Lincoln at the Hall of Presidents so that he shaves off his beard instead of freeing the slaves, ask the kids what they liked best. They will say the hotel's chicken nuggets.

Answer: Next time, give them that box the fridge came in and tell them it's Paris.

The Futility of Threats

You may have heard other parents say these things to their kids when they were on vacation:

"If you don't behave, we're going back home!"

"Settle down right now, or we're flying back three days early!"

"We've had just about enough! If you can't act like human beings we're checking out of the hotel RIGHT THIS INSTANT!"

We hate to break this to you, but your kids are not stupid. They know you CAN'T go home early. You're on a charter.

13

Your Children's Friends

(Or: Why you shouldn't lose one of them during a trip to the zoo)

If there's one thing we know for sure about how you as a father feel about your child, it's this: YOUR kid is the smartest, cutest, most polite, charming youngster on the entire planet.

Everybody ELSE'S kid is a slug.

This is something that you, as a father, come to realize very early in your child's life. Your child is without fault. And all the other parents should hang their heads in shame.

Even if your kid looks as though she may have inherited her good looks from living too close to a substandard nuclear facility; even if, when asked what two and two is, she says "green"; even if she tends to bruise easily during heated Parcheesi matches, you will view her as nothing short of beautiful and brilliant, a competitor with the killer instinct. You will love to play with her, to take her with you wherever you go, and show off to your coworkers the latest roll of pictures of her you've had developed.

You will be one proud papa.

This does not mean, however, that you love children. It just means that you love YOUR child.

But you will continue to view other people's kids in the same way you did before you had one of your own. Without exception, you will consider them noisy, rambunctious, snot-encrusted, ill-mannered, annoying, totally unnecessary creatures.

Before children, when you sat in a fast-food restaurant and the children at the next table were strangling each other over the last French fry, you would ask yourself: "Can their parents not SEE what's going on? Can they not CONTROL these savages?"

But now, sitting in this same restaurant with your own children, who are emptying ketchup packets onto each other's heads, putting fries into most (but, fortunately, not quite ALL) of their orifices, and wadding up paper napkins into pellets that can be blown through straws, you are completely consumed with the behavior of a child at the next table who has failed to say thank you when her mother gives her a Happy Meal, and pondering the total collapse of Western civilization.

The fact that fathers are blind to their own children's shortcomings, but acutely aware of those in others, can make life trying for dads who constantly find their homes overrun with the progeny of others.

But you better get used to it. All the experts (and if we could have found one to write this book, we would have, but the kids were always on the phone discussing Jonathan Taylor Thomas's hair, so we had to forget it) say that if you want to keep tabs on what your kids are up to, you must open up your home to their friends. Make them feel welcome, encourage them to hang out there.

Let's face it. If, on a Friday night, your kids and their noisy buddies are in your rec room, whooping it up and spraying each other with cans of pop they've been shaking for 25 minutes, at least you know where they ARE.

And once you DO know this, and are confident that they're in a safe, wholesome, nurturing environment, and that you or your wife can walk in on them at any moment on the pretext of saying you're just on the way to the laundry room, you can tell your spouse you're going to go out to get them a pizza, and not actually return until Sunday night.

Assessing Your Child's Peers

What set of criteria should you use to judge your children's friends?

First of all, are they aware that you exist?

Many of your children's playmates may seem incapable of acknowledging that you are a living, breathing, human adult.

When one arrives at your house, and you, in a bid to portray yourself as one of the more affable parents on the block, say something like "Hi there, Annette! How are you?" she will charge past you in a blur as she and your daughter race downstairs to trade stories about which of their best friends they hate the most that day.

All you may be looking for is a simple "Hi!" but you should not expect it. You are a parent. You are invisible. You will find this is still the case when you are fixing your child and her friend a snack in the kitchen:

"There you go, milk and cookies."
" _____ "

"I sure hope you LIKE those milk and cookies."
" _____ "

"That's really FRESH milk and those cookies contain a higher-than-average chip count, according to standards that have been set by the National Chocolate Chip Standards Council."
" _____ "

"You might be interested to know that your parents phoned a little while ago to say they're moving away and aren't going to tell you where they're going."
" _____ "

Next, you want to know that your children's friends are well-behaved and, especially when they're under your roof, respectful of other people's property.

> *Your child's friend:* Whoa, awesome, is this your Dad's computer?
> *Your child:* Yeah. This is the one he's writing his stupid book about fathers on.
> *Your child's friend:* Neat! Hey, I learned this real neat way to delete tons of files in seconds so you've got way more room for games. Wanna see?
> *Your child:* Oh, that is so COOL! Look at all the room that's been freed up on the hard drive!

And do they engage in language that you consider inappropriate? Eavesdrop on your child and her playmate to see if they're using words, and discussing issues, you take a dim view of.

> *Your child's friend:* Me and my family are having to take a lot of CRAP from the people next door about our pit bull after it ate their cousin visiting from Pennsylvania, and I think it really SUCKS that my dad doesn't get along with my mom's boyfriend, and my brother's really BUMMED OUT over his drug bust.
> *You: (bursting into the room)* That's "My family and I," young lady!

And last, but by no means least, what kind of values do they hold?

Are they in sync with your own? You might, for example, make your living as a government lobbyist. What if your kid starts hanging around with a child who has strong interests in baseball cards, science fiction movies, and the importance of empowering the individual against the interests of multinational corporations?

What are you going to do about a kid like that? You're going to tell your own child not to play with him, that's what.

But you also have to recognize that you can't always control who your children play with. You can't watch them 24 hours a day, even if, as that lobbyist, you have access to some of the finest surveillance firms in the country who've compiled some high-quality resolution photos of our elected officials in compromising positions with yaks.

So the best you can do is *guide* your child. Suggest to your children who, among their classmates, might make good playmates.

"You know, that Lionel boy, HE seems like a mighty nice kid."

"Dad, he licks toads."

"So he has an appreciation of wildlife. Did you know that his mother happens to be a member of the judiciary committee?"

"Daaaad, every time you dare him to stick his tongue to the frozen bike rack, he does it. His tongue looks like Velcro. He has the IQ of a TetraPak."

"Why don't you have him over after school one day?"

Considering that you may have limited success in picking for your child the friends you'd like him to have, you must be vigilant in watching for signs of bad influences.

For example, if your grade school daughter wants to cancel her official membership in the Baby-Sitters Club in order to devote herself more fully to her duties with a local association of devil worshipers, you may begin to wonder just where she's been getting her ideas.

Similarly, if your son's interests appear to have taken a dark turn, you may want to know more about the group he hangs out with. Consider, for example, the following list.

Ten signs your Grade 4 youngster is hanging out with a bad crowd

1. Has been awarded the contract to take out Barney.
2. Needs bigger allowance to cover higher costs for milk at

lunch, three-hole binders, and table dancers.

3. Has started carrying a beeper even though he does not yet have his real-estate license.
4. Has stopped saying "Neat!" and now says "Bitchin!"
5. Is only kid you know who has his own bail bondsman's card.
6. When a story comes on the radio about a strange series of squirrel stranglings in a nearby town, he pipes up: "I had nothing to do with it!"
7. Has pictures of his teacher naked. With the principal. And a ledger, showing monthly payments of $25 from the two of them, going back to the beginning of the school year.
8. Says not to bother packing him a lunch; he and his friends have a table at Luigi's.
9. Wants to get out of this Saturday's T-ball tournament to attend a body-piercing convention.
10. Has taken down his Tiny Toon posters and replaced them with Benetton ads.

Making the Best of It

You might as well accept the fact that your children are going to have friends, and that your involvement is paramount if you're to have any chance of knowing what's going on in their lives outside the home.

One way to do this is to let your child bring a friend on an excursion. This could be something as simple as a trip to the local bowling alley, or as ambitious as a day at a theme park or the zoo or an overnight camping adventure. There's no question it will be an endurance test for you, but it'll mean the world to your child.

Decide on a manageable number of friends for your kid to bring along on one of these trips.

You don't want to have more children than you can realistically keep track of, because (and we cannot overstate this) it's very important that you return with the same number of children you headed off with. You'll score even more points if they're the SAME children you left with.

Do regular head counts. (But as we know from the movie *Home Alone*, where the parents had the right NUMBER of people in the van that would take them to the airport, but not necessarily the right PEOPLE, this is not always adequate. You must familiarize yourself with the actual faces of those children who are in your charge.)

You might want to consider name tags, or, if the kids are young enough, hooking them together in a leash-like fashion so that no one gets away without your knowing about it.

If you have access to high-tech parole service equipment, you might want to fit them all with electronic bracelets that monitor their positions at all times by satellite.

These kinds of precautions are worth the effort, because losing one of your child's friends is a major *faux pas*, one that you should strive to avoid — even if it brings about the unintended, but not altogether unpleasant, consequence that not another parent in the neighborhood will ever let his kid play at your house again.

14

The Tossing of Cookies

(Or: "I wouldn't step there if I were you")

Warning: Portions of this chapter deal with mature, sensitive, and somewhat slippery subject matter.

Despite the title of this chapter, many of you have probably already guessed that we are not referring here to some cute lunchtime game or a baking exercise. We are not talking baseball with biscuits.

We are talking about the launching into the atmosphere of previously eaten food particles before they have completed the digestive process.

You will probably have some familiarity with this topic even before you become a father, especially if you were on your college's rowing or rugby team. You may even be familiar with the notion of another person depositing a previously consumed 2–4 on your shoes, but it's not until you become a father that you realize this kind of thing can happen at any time, without warning.

When you were in college, it was an *objective*. Now it becomes a *surprise*.

Despite how often this topic touches our lives personally, there is not nearly as much research on it as you might think.

However, there is some very exciting work underway at the Hurling Academy of Boston, which found that children's vomit operates according to several natural principles, outlined in the following list.

☆

The Six Basic Principles of Vomit

1. There's no better place than a fine restaurant.
2. It may smell like Parmesan cheese, but it is no substitute.
3. Given a choice between tile and carpet, vomit will always gravitate to carpet.
4. Similar results have been found with car upholstery (vomit preferring luxurious velour upholstery to cheap vinyl).
5. The toilet is always two steps too far away.
6. Vomit will usually have its operator (the child) notify parents that it's on the way before one of the following functions: (a) bar mitzvah, (b) wedding, (c) Christmas dinner, (d) arrival of the school bus, (e) sex.

There are a few other things you should know about a child who says she is going to be sick to her stomach. Don't think, even for a minute, that you can stop this from happening. There is no point in offering a bribe.

"I'll give you two dollars if you don't throw up. Here, just take the money and — oh dear. I wish I'd given that to you in coins."

Also, ask your child lots of questions if he tells you that his tummy isn't feeling well. Often the first thing an incredibly stupid father assumes is: "Listen, you're probably just HUNGRY! Let me make you something to eat."

The child, who is not yet old enough to understand some of the signals his stomach is sending to his brain, may actually think his

103

father is right, and will sit down to three hot dogs, four Cokes, and a bag of chips before realizing that, no, hunger is definitely NOT the problem.

Getting new wallpaper, that's what the problem's going to be.

Situations to Avoid

Certain kinds of situations can easily lend themselves to episodes of vomiting. If you're aware of what they are ahead of time, you have a better chance of avoiding unpleasant moments.

All you have to do is make a note of the following, extremely rare, particularly high-risk activities and make sure your child does not engage in them:

- running
- walking
- going to birthday parties
- eating junk food
- eating healthy food
- riding in a car
- playing video games
- going to school
- staying home from school
- going up stairs too fast
- going up stairs too slow
- playing
- sitting in a chair doing absolutely nothing
- trick-or-treating at Halloween
- watching Polka Dot Door

In particular you'll want to avoid events where the amount of available food is unlimited. Buffet dinners, weddings, parties, the launching of a new car dealership: these should be avoided at all costs.

Take, for example, the church supper. Here is the story of one Wilbur Thickweed, father, from Norwood, Ontario:

"We were at a church supper, one of those summer get-togethers where they prepare a Christmas-type dinner, with turkey and dressing and potatoes and rolls. There was a large cooler set up to dispense orange pop for the kids.

"I suppose I could have been paying better attention and headed this off, but my son Jason kept going back for more and more cups of pop. This, combined with piles of turkey and gravy and rolls and lemon meringue pie, led to a mighty undesirable result. He turned to me as they were clearing up the dishes and said: 'Dad, I don't feel too good.' And I'll tell ya, he didn't LOOK none too good.

"I think if they'd built the washrooms 30 feet closer to where we were sitting, or if we'd taken a table just a little closer to them, we might have made it. As it turned out, Jason slapped his fingers over his mouth to try to keep it all in, but I tell ya, it was like a dam bursting, just as we walked into the men's room, all this orange stuff came spewing out between us and the stalls, narrowly missing a guy standing at the urinal.

"We had the equivalent of an oil slick between us and the stalls, and it was pretty clear there wasn't much need to get to them now, but Jason wanted to try anyway, but you see, we had to step THROUGH the oil slick to get to the stalls, and when we did, well, it made me think that maybe we should have invested a little more in skating lessons for the lad.

"There was arms flyin' in the air, his head was spinnin' around, and then his legs was out from under him and SPLAT there he was right in the midst of it. You'd think he'd been dunked in a can of orange paint."

Thinking Fast in an Emergency

Here are 10 things you can do in a crowded Chinese food restaurant on Mother's Day after your five-year-old daughter, whom you've already told seven times to settle down, sticks a chopstick down the back of her throat and deposits her entire dinner all over the table:

1. Call your waiter over and tell him you don't know why, but the soo gai seems to be spreading.
2. Announce that you are a health inspector and this is a raid.
3. Mutter loud enough for the patrons at the nearby tables to hear you: "Oh, that darn MSG."
4. Tell your wife you're just going to check that the parking meter hasn't expired, and spend the rest of the day looking at drill bits at your local hardware store.
5. Introduce the members of your family to the people at the next table, finishing with your daughter: "And, of course, you know Linda Blair."
6. Ask your waiter if you can be seated at another table because when you sat down at yours, it was covered with vomit. Have a good reason why you didn't notice this until your fourth course.
7. Tell your wife that you and the kids just wanted to make this a Mother's Day she'd never forget.
8. Lean over to the table next to you, cough, and say: "Whew, that Ebola virus, it's somethin', huh?"
9. Say to your waiter: "Listen, forget the fortune cookies, just bring us the check."
10. Tip REALLY well.

On the Home Front

As you can tell from the stories above, if your child vomits in a public place, it can be tremendously embarrassing, but at least there's the benefit that you won't have to clean it up.

Accidents in the home, however, are a different matter.

When your child has the flu, we recommend giving him the red carpet treatment. But it's not really carpet, but towels. And they don't have to be red.

Use bath towels to create a pathway from the child's bed to the bathroom door. The reason for this is simple: a child's stomach does not usually send a message to the child's brain that it is about to erupt until it has already blown the peak off the top of the mountain.

That means the child has generally only made it halfway to the bathroom before horrifying things start to happen. The towels will help protect your carpeting.

The only possible way this can go wrong is if your child's stomach doesn't bother sending any messages to the brain at all, in which case you will have to change all the bedding.

If your child says his stomach feels upset, and that it would actually be a relief to throw up, you can help things along without the purchase of any over-the-counter medications.

Simply put on your best suit, an Armani shirt, and a $90 Hugo Boss tie, and then pick your child up. This works every time.

Trying to Keep Stomach Flu Out of Your House

Good luck. Here's a typical example of what you're up against.

You and another parent have arranged for your kids to get together for an afternoon of play. This can be great, because a home with two children in it can often be a lot quieter than a home with one bored child in it. Any parent will tell you that if your youngster has a buddy over, you can get a ton of things done around the house.

But your plans for an afternoon of productivity can be overshadowed by anxiety if, when your friend drops off his kid, he says:

"Well, she was puking her guts out all night and she threw up when she got up this morning, but she hasn't thrown up for the last half hour so I'm sure she's fine and she was so looking forward to playing with your little Angela that I couldn't bear to disappoint her and boy it's so good of you to take her, I'm going to get a round of golf in, see ya later, and good luck with Angela's communion tomorrow, I hear all your relatives are flying in from Calgary."

Your friend's little girl promptly goes over and gives your daughter Angela a big kiss right on the mouth.

But everything works out great, because your daughter doesn't actually start throwing up the next day until everyone's back from the church. It's unfortunate, however, that she chooses to do it right into the vegetable lasagna.

15

Making Time

(Or: How to read a newspaper)

Fathers of the '90s have it a lot tougher than many are willing to admit ("many" being a clever code word for "women").

While it's true women have been undergoing horrendous stresses as well, the difference is that attention is being paid to their plight, particularly on the covers of women's magazines, which have for years been carrying headlines like "Superwomen: How Do They Do It?"; "The Sandwich Generation"; "Balancing Career and Family"; and "The 75-Hour Orgasm," which is another thing that has really got the guys cheesed off.

But magazines geared to more traditionally male interests have totally ignored this problem. Cover stories like "The Robertson Screwdriver: Here to Stay or Just a Passing Fad?" and "How to Drink Beer Safely While Lying Down" add little to the much-needed debate about the pressures modern fathers face.

As we reach the end of this century, fathers are finding they're running out of time where their own families are concerned. There aren't enough hours in the day for them to meet all the demands placed upon them from the home and the workplace.

In this recession-ravaged decade, men with children have constantly had to sacrifice their home life to ensure that they not only continue to bring in a good salary, but remain employed at all.

Boss: Smithers, I want you to take a look at this file on the Disney–ABC–Department of National Defense–CBC–Westinghouse–Time-Warner–NASA–McDonald's–Seagram's–Miss Vickie's Potato Chips merger and have a report on my desk first thing in the morning suggesting what course of action we should take, even though it has nothing to do with us, considering that we just make those little hard things that go on the end of shoelaces, whatever they're called.

Employee: Well gee, boss, I'd really like to, but I'm going to my daughter's ballet recital tonight, and I haven't actually SEEN her since February and my wife says I won't believe how she's grown and I only hope I recognize her but she IS the only one who's doing an interpretive dance of the "Oswald acted alone" theory, so I SHOULD be able to spot her —

Boss: *(quickly punching his intercom)* Bring in the "dozens-of-unemployed-single-guys-without-children-eager-to-make-a-name-for-themselves-by-working-selflessly-until-they-have-a-heart-attack-before-they're-23" file!

Employee: Just let me make a call.

Some fathers get to work so early in the morning and home so late at night that the only time they actually see their children is when the kids are asleep, or on weekends, when they are much too busy trying out the new riding lawnmower to really connect with their offspring.

Of course, those at the higher end of the corporate food chain, like big-shot executives and CEOs of major corporations, who can delegate much of these responsibilities, have had it a little easier.

Big Shot: Ms. Featherstone, what are the names of my children again?

Secretary: There's Amy, who's ten, Roger, who's seven, and little Amanda, who's three days old now and doing just fine.

Big Shot: Oh yes, that rings a bell. That would explain why my wife was in hospital.

Secretary: Yes, sir. The delivery went very well, sir. It was an honor to be there to help her with the breathing exercises.

Big Shot: Do send yourself a little something as a thank-you. And get a nice card, and sign it "With deepest gratitude, your boss." Something like that.

Secretary: You do think of everything, sir.

Of course, it can still be argued that we make our choices in life, and that a father who chooses career over family only has himself to blame when, years later, upon showing up at his grown daughter's house for Thanksgiving dinner, he is given the boot because he hasn't brought along any ID to prove he's who he says he is.

To ward off this kind of thing happening, many of today's dads are looking at alternatives, like job-sharing, working out of the home, early retirement, or the following novel approach, which you will probably be reading about here for the very first time.

The "Faddy"

All that you've read so far goes a long way to explaining the growing popularity of the "faddy," for "fake daddy."

Modeled on the nanny concept, more and more faddies are being hired by families where the children have a strong paternal need, but the father is so consumed with duties outside the home he simply doesn't have enough time to be there.

A faddy complements the services already being provided by a nanny, who, in most cases, will be working in the household through the day. The faddy steps in later, at a time of the day when one might normally have expected a father to have arrived.

The duties of a faddy include:

- coming in the front door at the appointed hour, shouting "I'm home," and acting completely oblivious to the fact that no one seems to care
- going through that day's mail, and upon seeing the bills, grumbling things like: "Oh for the love of! Who's been using so much hot water? And this HEAT bill! What is this, the tropics? We're turning back that thermostat starting TONIGHT, mark my words!"
- asking why it is that he's the only one in the entire household qualified to bring in the empty trash cans and recycling boxes from the curb
- asking children at dinner what they learned in school and then regaling them with supposedly amusing but totally pointless stories about his own days in the public school system (it doesn't matter whether these stories are the real father's or the faddy's, since no one will be listening)
- after dinner, putting away various pots and pans and dishes in all the wrong places, as though this was the very first time he'd ever been in this kitchen, even though you have lived there for 17 years
- driving kids to early morning hockey practices, being sure to always back over a tricycle (applicants should have their own car)

Needless to say, when this kind of high-level expertise is what's required, finding a properly qualified faddy is not easy. But nor is it impossible.

There are a growing number of agencies where you can find a faddy. Word of mouth is also highly recommended, or you can always just grab the first guy you see walking by on the sidewalk.

The interview process is absolutely crucial in finding a suitable candidate. You and your wife should sit down with each applicant and quiz him thoroughly about his background, just as you would with a new nanny or babysitter.

Dad: Now, it says here you've completed your postsecondary degree in Paternal Emulation.
Candidate: That's correct.
Dad: And you're familiar with most of the basics — playing catch, fixing stuck drawers, putting together doll houses, getting balls off the roof.
Candidate: Absolutely.
Dad: You know, it's funny. Do people ever tell you that you look exactly like Mel Gibson?
Candidate: All the time.
Mother: I think you're going to work out just fine. You're hired.
Dad: Well, I did have a couple more ques—
Mother: Shut up.

As you can see from this exchange, there can be drawbacks in hiring a faddy, not the least of which is your family will come to prefer him to you.

If you hire a faddy who looks as though he just walked off the set of a Fox-TV prime-time soap, you may find your wife more and more understanding when you phone from the office to say that you're going to be late once again.

"Look, I'm really sorry. Maybe you can get the faddy to cover for me."

"No need to apologize," your wife will say. "We'll try to — *hee, hee! don't touch me there, it tickles! —* manage."

Dealing with the Guilt

You might have thought it was only women who feel guilty when work keeps them away from their children. But men feel pretty miserable, too.

113

The sexes, however, have different methods of dealing with this guilt. Women will search for ways to spend more time with their children, even if it means sneaking out of work early to race across town to meet them coming out of school, or staying up late on the eve of a child's birthday to make cupcakes for the entire class, even though she has a 7 a.m. meeting that could make or break her career.

Men, on the other hand, deal with their guilt somewhat differently. They reach into their wallets.

If you've been working long hours for weeks on end, involved in important research that will have a lasting beneficial impact on mankind, like coming up with a new jingle for underarm deodorant, and your kids have started complaining, try buying them off.

Bring home gifts. Video games, building sets, dolls, books, candy, whatever it takes. After a while, your children may start resenting your trying to buy their affection. If this happens, buy them even more stuff.

Dad: And what do I have here? Could it be a Veronica Vomit doll, the ONLY doll on the market who's bulimic —

Daughter: Daaaddd. You just can't keep buying me things as a way of making me feel better that you're never home these days.

Dad: — WITH a full line of accessories, including her own totally waterproof purse for those times when she can't get to a ladies room!

Daughter: Ooooh, awesome.

The Reverse Problem

For dads who are really committed to spending extra time with their children, the trick can actually be finding some time for themselves. Sometimes even the simplest of things can become a luxury.

Take reading the paper, for example.

Finding a few moments of quiet time to catch up on the events of the day can often be as challenging as raising kids. If there are frequent interruptions, a father may find himself reading the same thing over and over again.

Here is how the average father reads a story in his daily newspaper:

> TORONTO (CP) Researchers have found that the atten-
> tion span of the average —

"Dad! Dad? Dad! I can't find my turtle! He was right here in his little bowl but now he isn't. Can you please help me find him? PLEASE?"

Twenty minutes later:

> TORONTO (CP) Researchers have found that the atten-
> tion span of the average male is now —

"Oh, Dad? Martin won't stay out of my room! I've told him to stay out of my room but he's just standing here and he's really starting to annoy me, especially when he puts on his goalie mask and starts up his chain saw!"

"Martin! Martin? Get out of your sister's room! And turn off that goldarned chain saw, I can hardly hear myself think down here!"

> TORONTO (CP) Researchers have found that the atten-
> tion span of the average male is now only 17 seconds, but
> in fathers of school-age children, that actually drops to —

"Dad, I'm having a bit of trouble with this question on my homework? And I was wondering? Like, if you could help me? For a second? If you're not too busy?"

"Go ahead."

"It's all about punctuation? And what you should put at the end of a sentence? And when you should use a question mark? And when you shouldn't? Do you know what I mean?"

Thirty minutes later:

TORONTO (CP) Researchers have found that the attention span of the average male is now only 17 seconds, but in fathers of school-age children, that actually drops to a unit of time that scientists have so far been unable to measure.

"We found," said the research project leader, "that fathers who were unable to find a moment's peace often erupted in unpredictable, horrific bursts of —

"Dad!"

16

Craft-Making

(Or: "The horror. The horror.")

Children will often come to you, especially on those gray days when there's nothing to do, with the question: "Can we do some crafts?"

As you probably know, craft-making is a terrific pastime for youngsters.

It challenges them creatively and mentally. It improves their small motor skills and helps them develop artistic sensibilities that can last their entire lives. It is a very educational form of play that's certainly much better for a child than watching television.

Avoid it at all costs.

Craft-making is the messiest, most potentially disastrous activity a small child can engage in under your roof. And trying to dissuade your child from being interested in it is like asking Madonna to concentrate on making some really good albums. You are wasting your breath.

Children's crafts are a multi-billion dollar industry exceeding the

117

GNP of several of the smaller nations, like Germany. There are rows upon rows devoted to them at your local Toys "R" Us. Several children's television programs show them how to make crafts. There are dozens of books on the market with thousands of craft ideas. It's all part of the huge conspiracy to rob parents of whatever free time they foolishly thought they had left.

You see, contrary to the popular belief that crafts keep CHILDREN busy, what they really do is occupy millions of parental hours setting up, supervising, and cleaning up.

Take a simple commercially available craft, Doozy Daffodils, only $34.95, which allows your small children to make beautiful paper flowers.

All you have to do is punch out the petal shapes from the Doozy Daffodils colored sheets, work them through the plastic flower petal presser (comes in Petunia Pink or Mauve Marigold!), feeding in the end of the sheet marked "B" into the petal presser sleeve marked "A," then crank one half turn, fold sheet back carefully along dotted line "D" and twist counter-clockwise into slot "F." Finally, turn your head to the side and cough.

These types of craft toys are known throughout the industry as PFMs, or "Parental Frustration Machines." No adult, let alone child, has ever been able to make one of these infernal things produce flowers or fashion accessories or little rubber creepy crawlers as easily as they're done on the Saturday morning commercials.

One way to know, in fact, whether the parents of your child's friends hate you is if they give your child a craft toy for her birthday.

This is their way of saying: "We've already got enough friends for bridge, so why don't you stay home and have some quality time with your kids? *Ha ha ha!*"

Most crafts, however, can be created with common household items. Not only is this less expensive than buying a craft toy, but it's actually a form of recycling, which is a very '90s thing to do.

With homemade crafts, instead of throwing out tin cans and cardboard and apple juice bottles, you hang on to them for several weeks, not throwing them out until they're gunged up with several coats of glue, paint, and boogers, thereby rendering them totally useless to the recycling industry.

Craft Alternatives

For mothers and fathers who like a neat, tidy house, a child embarking on a craft-making exercise can be as exciting as hearing news reports that a Force Five hurricane is bearing down on your neighborhood.

For example, craft-making is the only activity where you will ever be asked the following questions.

1. "Mommy, I was making this really pretty collage thing and I wanted to know if it's okay that I cut up a bit of that old fancy white dress with the veil that you had in a box in the top of the closet that you said you only wore once anyway?"

2. "Can Johnny's dad come and pick him up now? Ever since I dared him to lick the top of the Krazy Glue tube, he's refused to talk to me."

3. "Can you come see the great Play-Doh thing I made by turning the CD player into a mold?"

If your child comes to you on a rainy day and demands construction paper and scissors, some torn-up newspaper, 4,000 multi-colored plastic beads, white glue, a stapler, pipe cleaners, elbow macaroni, a glue gun, popsicle sticks, Krazy Glue, red and green and blue glitter, and carpenter's glue, attempt to steer her interests in another direction.

Here are just a few children's activities that are less stressful for parents than craft-making:

- reading
- talking to a friend on the phone

- playing computer games
- joining a neighborhood gang
- working at a 24-hour gas bar in a bad part of town
- teasing a leopard
- welding

Some Good Craft Projects

If your child is bound and determined to make a craft, there's little you can do. Besides, there's nothing that makes you feel more guilty than stifling your child's creativity. So pick a good spot where a little mess won't matter.

A few good locations are your child's friend's house, a tennis court, the roof of the local high school, and Saskatchewan. There are huge tracts of Saskatchewan that nobody's putting to any good use, and a little spilled glue or paint isn't going to make any difference to anyone.

Here are a few less chaotic craft-making projects for your child.

Fold a piece of paper: Take a sheet of 8 x 11 paper, and instruct your child to fold it in half, either vertically or horizontally. Make a big fuss when this is done. Stick it to the fridge, and tell him to go play outside.

Make a toilet paper tube: This is not only tremendously creative play for youngsters, but it helps with their counting skills. Hand your child a roll of toilet paper and tell him to count off each sheet as he tears it off until he reaches the cardboard "telescope" hidden inside.

Build a twig: Get your child in touch with nature, or at the very least, a shrub. Have him break off a short branch and imagine that it's a space ship. (This only works with very small children, like under 6 months. Any older, and they're likely to respond with that cute, impish rejoinder: "Get stuffed.")

Disposing of Crafts

Little boys and girls like to save every single drawing and craft item they have ever made. In other words, they are exactly like their mothers, who will look at a red paper heart stuck to a piece of green construction paper with the aid of three pounds of kindergarten paste and, while weeping uncontrollably, proclaim that it's the most beautiful thing they've ever seen.

Fathers, on the other hand, will smile and nod approvingly and then figure out how to get rid of it before the dog eats it.

But there comes a time when even the most sentimental parents — fathers AND mothers — reach the point when they realize they're going to have to do something about the mountain of crafts that's taking over their lives.

If you are not sure whether you've reached that point, take the following quiz:

1. Do you no longer park your car in the garage because it's taken up entirely with empty fridge crates converted into clubhouses, a life-size papier-mâché reproduction of the Ice Fortress from Superman, and a Batmobile made entirely of tomato rotini?
2. Do you sneak down to the kitchen in the dead of night to throw out the empty Cheerios, Frosted Flakes, and Froot Loops boxes that have been taking up valuable cupboard space, just so the kids won't spot you doing it and ask for them so they can make Seaquest submarine control panels?
3. Is your living room carpet no longer visible because it's buried under two inches of Styrofoam packing noodles that the kids have gone door to door collecting?
4. Do your children forbid you to put big plastic pop bottles in the recycling bin because, once joined together with duct tape, they make great pretend diving tanks? And do you now

have enough diving equipment to equip the entire U.S. Navy for a raid on Cuba?

If you answered yes to all four of these questions, not only is it time for you to take action, but you should also seriously consider therapy.

What to do? Reasonable mothers and fathers can explain to their children, forcefully if necessary, that there's simply no way all of these things can be saved, that you ALL have to live in this house together, INCLUDING the parents, and the kids will have to pick the few crafts that really mean a lot to them, and the rest are going to have to go into the trash.

But seeing as how reasonable parents who know how to deal with their children in a logical and effective manner constitute a statistically insignificant part of the population, there are other methods of dealing with this.

Have Your Home Burglarized

All you need to do here is hire someone to break into your house while you're away (WITH THE KIDS, it hardly needs to be pointed out, so as to provide you with an alibi).

Hiring people for this type of work is not as difficult as you might think. Type up a note similar to the one pictured below, then post it on your local grocery store's bulletin board, with plenty of tear-off phone numbers.

> **Desperate parents require services of break-in artist to deal with CRAFT OVERLOAD!**
>
> ☆
>
> No experience necessary but record of insurance fraud a definite asset.
> Must supply own truck.

It should be noted that this kind of approach is not without risk. No matter how extensively you brief your burglar with a complete description of your children's crafts, there's still a chance that he'll make off with your Mark Rothko poster and knickknacks from the Art Gallery of Ontario because he couldn't tell the difference.

Sell Them
Conversely, if your hired burglar can't tell the difference between modern art and your kids' cardboard and pasta creations, maybe the National Gallery in Ottawa can't either.

Give them a call one day when the kids are at school and tell them you are acting on behalf of noted Bolivian artist Gustav Phlegm, whose work, they must SURELY realize, has skyrocketed in value ever since that ghastly accident Gustav had with his family's dairy farm milking machine.

You'll have a representative of the museum carting off the stuff before your children are home from school, but they won't be crying when you tell them you wangled enough money from the federally funded gallery to buy them 25 popsicles, 10 action figures, a dozen packs of baseball cards, and the Toronto-Dominion bank tower in the heart of the city's financial district.

Move
This may strike some parents as extreme, but when you figure there's always a chance that the movers could lose some of your belongings, it's worth a shot.

Environmental Hazards
Enlist the aid of your local office of the ministry of the environment to have your children's excess crafts declared toxic waste.

Your kids will be the envy of the other neighborhood children when that white van pulls up in the drive and six men in hermetically sealed space suits make their way through the house disposing of old egg cartons converted into Barbie recording studios, reproductions of Renaissance period masterpieces done in pencil shavings and dog hair, and the kids' very own frog autopsy kit made from discarded shoe boxes.

17

Tidying

(Or: How to pick up a sock)

As a loving, compassionate caring dad, which of the following things do you say when you step through the door of your home to greet your loving family after a harrowing, stressful, gruelling day at work?

   a) "Who left their bikes and skateboards and hockey sticks all over the driveway?"
   b) "Someone go out there NOW and clean up that mess of candy wrappers, melted crayons, baseball cards, and unused chicken parts in the backseat of my car!"
   c) "Honey, I'm home!"

If you picked (c) you are not a real person, but a fictional character in a television sitcom. You're not real, your dog isn't real, and your family isn't real, which should have dawned on you earlier since your kids have names like Biff, Wally, and Susie.

Learning that you do not really exist comes as a blow to some but it can be a tremendous relief when the Visa statement arrives. "Hey," you can say, "why should I pay this if I'm just a figment of some bozo scriptwriter's imagination?"

However, if you picked (a) or (b), you can rest comfortably in the knowledge that you are a real, honest-to-goodness, whining, grouchy, miserable father who understands that hounding his kids about leaving X-Men figures, Lego pieces, damp towels, and dirty laundry all over the house builds character, teaches children responsibility, and drives them to get a place of their own by the time they're 11.

How Children Get This Way

It's hard to understand where children get their bad habits — at least, until you take a look at your own bedroom, workshop, or garage.

For example, chances are very good that your toolbox contains some of the following things:

- 624 rusty screws of assorted types and sizes
- 7 different, already opened packs of faucet washers, each with one washer missing
- an old, two-pronged multi-outlet electrical plug, which you've been hanging onto just in case grounded, three-pronged plugs prove to be a passing fad
- some weird-looking clamp that looks suspiciously like it came from a store called "Wanda's Pleasure Chest"
- 4 almost totally disintegrated pieces of fine sanding paper
- 3 concrete drill bits you borrowed from your neighbor in 1987 and now don't have the nerve to return
- a 1976 AMC Pacer key fob
- 13 pipe elbows you REMOVED when you had leaks in the house, but now hang onto just in case you'd ever like to upgrade your plumbing with defective fittings

Now, if you could look inside the brain of a small child and examine the part that looks after tidiness, it would look very similar to the inside of your toolbox.

But instead of pipe fittings and washers and sandpaper, you'd find Barbie shoes, used Lion King bandages, pieces of colored cardboard made to look like various household appliances and instruments of torture, pen caps, Gargoyle Pogs, and Hot Wheels cars that change color when you run them under hot water.

There is no order here, only chaos, and the sooner you learn to deal with it, the less risk you have of a heart attack before you turn 40.

How Children Get Distracted

Let's take a very simple case that shows how a small child handles the most basic of tidying tasks — picking up some dirty clothes.

Suppose you discover, just outside your child's bedroom door, a sock. You say to your child:

"Would you please pick up that sock and put it in the laundry hamper?"

First, you must determine whether the child, who is approximately seven feet away from you, lying on his bed reading a Batman comic, heard you.

You never know. There might have been a sonic boom that you missed, or a small earthquake you failed to notice. Perhaps a dog was barking outside, and it somehow interfered with your child being able to interpret your instructions.

"Hey, did you hear me? Would you please pick up that sock?"

"Huh, what?"

"The sock. Would you please pick up that sock?"

The child, without even looking at the item of clothing, will ALWAYS respond: "That's not MY sock."

He knows he MAY get lucky. Sure, it's only five inches long, this sock, but MAYBE it belongs to his mother or father and just shrunk, or MAYBE it belongs to his sister or another sibling.

But had he looked at it, he would have known that this was no regular white or blue or black sock, but a Wolverine sock, and there is no one in the house who would choose to wear a Wolverine sock but him.

So you say, in your most lawyerly parent voice:

"I didn't ask you whose sock it was, I asked you to pick it up and put it in the dirty clothes basket. And besides, it IS your sock."

The child emits a sigh and exhibits some signs that he is going to comply with your request, so you go on about your business.[1]

Now the child fully intends, at this point, to pick up the sock, but something happens between getting off the bed and moving the two or three steps to where the sock is positioned on the floor. He becomes distracted. The following actual tape recording of a child's thoughts illustrates the problem:

"Sheesh, I'm always having to DO things around here, like I'm some sort of a SLAVE, like that time in *Star Trek*, where they made Kirk wear that collar thing around his neck so he'd have to do anything they wanted him to do like take over the ship which reminds me where's *my* Enterprise which I THOUGHT was in my room but I haven't seen up here and my rotten little sister better not have been playing with it so I'm going to check her room right now, that miserable rotten little thief."

The child is then heard banging around in his sister's room, rummaging about in the bottom of her closet, yanking open drawers, upending her toy basket and spilling out her Polly Pocket

---

[1]Children's sighs are one of our nation's greatest untapped sources of energy. Studies by various federal departments of natural resources have shown that a typical child gives off seven sighs a day, each one having, on average, enough force to power a windmill for 1.5 minutes. If these collective sighs could be harnessed, the experts say, it would drastically reduce our dependence on foreign oil. And if you add in that guy at work, who rolls his eyes when you ask him to do anything, boy, you'd really be on to something.

collection, all 620 of the Little Sister books, 15 stuffed bunnies, and 96 of her 101 Dalmatians.

On your next pass by his door, you notice the sock is still where you first spotted it.

"Hey, what gives? Didn't I ask you to pick up this sock? And where are you?"

"I'm in here!" he shouts from his sister's room. "She stole my Enterprise!"

Upon entering your daughter's room you discover you've now got a much bigger mess on your hands than one stray sock.

"WHAT'S GOING ON IN HERE!!? WHAT HAVE YOU DONE TO YOUR SISTER'S THINGS?"

The child will now look around him, somewhat bewildered by the scene he has created. "Oh, I guess I better clean this up," he says, somewhat sheepishly.

"I should think SO!"

As the child puts the first dalmation back into the toy basket, he thinks: "Boy I hate her hate her hate her so MUCH for taking my Enterprise, she'll pay for this and I don't get it because she doesn't even LIKE Star Trek so I don't know why she'd take it and WAAAAIIT a minute I think I left it in Dad's workshop so I better go down and check there RIGHT NOW!"

By the time this process is completed, not only will your workshop and daughter's room be trashed, so will your garage, study, family room, kitchen, and laundry room. Your demand that the child pick up a sock, which is still on the floor where you first discovered it, has turned your residence into a location shoot for a made-for-TV movie about Hurricane Andrew.

The good thing this, you can come out of this having learned a valuable lesson: Next time, pick up the sock yourself.

(By the way, if you peek under that Toronto Raptors T-shirt wadded up on his bed, you'll find the Enterprise.)

How to Get Children to Clean Up Their Rooms

Forget it. There's nothing you can do to get your kids to clean up their rooms. Threats, bribery — absolutely nothing works. But there are some things you can do if you want your children's rooms to be neat and tidy for an upcoming special occasion, like a visit from the in-laws, perhaps, or a prospective buyer, since you've decided to put your house on the market after that little bit of unpleasantness with the neighbor, whose prized boa constrictor collection has been a bone of contention ever since the disappearance of Gunther, your dachshund.

These tidying steps include:

1. *Rent the SkyDome vacuum:* This is a terrific gadget that the stadium cleaning crews use to suck up several thousand pop containers, hot dog wrappers, baseball fans who've nodded off, and other trash after the end of each game.

If it can handle a job like that in just a few minutes, it should be able to clear out your child's room in a day or two. (Keep in mind

that this machine is rather large; it may be necessary to remove a section of roof to allow some of the attachments to squeeze inside.)

2. *Dynamite:* Admittedly a bit messy, but it does allow you to make a fresh start. One stick should do, but use more if it's a room shared by two or more siblings.

3. *Extra beds:* There's nothing like a bed, especially a queen- or king-sized one, for hiding a child's junk. Since the typical child can fill all the space under a single bed in a matter of minutes, you're going to need more.

Head over to Ikea and buy half a dozen more, or whatever it takes to cover every inch of floor space. Not only does this hide all the junk, but it's like turning the room into one giant trampoline.

(Avoid low-hanging light fixtures if you take this route.)

WARNING: Before trying any of these tidying steps, make sure that there aren't any missing members of your family already in there.

Most messy children's rooms take on the same properties as black holes and suck almost anything into them, never to be seen again.

Every year, you hear about tearful family reunions, like the one involving the Butler family, of Kenora, Ontario, who finally located their missing 64-year-old Aunt Hilda, who'd gone into her 7-year-old niece Patsy's room on December 24 and wasn't seen again until the following July 17.

That's when a construction crew came to install some new double-paned insulated windows, and heard some barely audible groaning from one corner of the little girl's bedroom.

Said the crew's foreman: "We found her buried under a mountain of Gund toys. She was a bit disoriented, and a little bit hungry. Apparently she'd lived on a diet of polyester fur and the odd half-empty juice box that got tossed back that way."

18

Sibling Rivalry

(Or: The nutritional value of the plastic spider hidden in the mashed potatoes)

Parents who have more than one child know that their kids have three fundamental needs:

1. The need for love and security.
2. The need for food and shelter.
3. The need to make life a living hell for their siblings, each and every moment of every day.

Psychologists differ on why this is. For example, the noted brother–sister team, Dr. Wayne Fitzgilder and Dr. Loretta Fitzgilder, at a recent international symposium into the mystery of sibling rivalry, made the following observations.

Dr. Wayne F.: The underlying roots of sibling conflict can be found in the process of self-affirmation. If you can provoke someone else, get a reaction, it reaffirms that you do, in fact, exist.
Dr. Loretta F.: Oh yeah, four-eyes?

It may be that fighting with a sibling is just another natural step in the maturation process, where children learn to assert their own authority, to stand up for themselves, to look out for Number One. In other words, it's a vitally important stage that prepares a child for adulthood and the working world, where it's so important to have the confidence to say: "Hey, that's not my job."

Whatever the reason, we do know that disagreements and outright fights between brothers and sisters have been going on since the dawn of time — even, in fact, before the Smothers Brothers.

Few know that the problems between Cain and Abel grew from something as innocent as a squabble over whose turn it was to help Mom make the apple crumble.

And few people realize that when Orville and Wilbur Wright were just kids, before they put their heads together to build the first airplane, Orville would often take Wilbur to the roof of their house, fit him with a specially made chicken-feather shirt, and say: "Go ahead, jump. I KNOW this is going to work."

(Wilbur waited until their famous flight at Kitty Hawk, North Carolina, to fully retaliate. Once the first airborne adventure was complete, Orville learned that Wilbur had his luggage sent to Cleveland.)

And what about the troubles between Romulus and Remus? Everybody knows Romulus could never find it in his heart to forgive his brother for not sharing any of the royalties he earned from his classic stories about Brer Rabbit and Brer Fox.

But it's comforting to know that many siblings who fight endlessly as children, who hate each other's guts with a passion and spend countless hours plotting revenge, who swear they will never, EVER, have anything to do with each other as adults, will often, once they grow up and have access to firearms, blow each other away on sight.

Fights Involving Ownership

In the basement, in one of those forgotten toy baskets on the shelf, is an old, retired, long-ignored Teenage Mutant Ninja Turtle figure — Donatello, perhaps — in which your son has shown no interest since the summer of 1991, when he placed it on the railroad tracks to see who'd win an encounter between an action figure and the 4:43 train.

Considering that your son has also performed several other sadistic experiments, without benefit of anesthetic, on Donatello (giving you mixed feelings about his comments that he'd like to pursue a career in medicine someday), it's pretty safe to assume this is no longer one of his most treasured playthings.

But on this particular day, his younger sister, rummaging around through the old toys trying to find Barbie a matching set of pumps, has come across the butchered and abused Donatello, and has brought him over to the Barbie house to play the role of Donny, Ken's extremely accident-prone little brother with the terrible skin condition.

Once your son discovers this, all hell breaks loose.

"DAAAAAAAAAAADDDDDDDD!" he screams, in a voice guaranteed to have the neighbors dialing 911. "SHE'S PLAYING WITH MY TOYS!"

The experienced, insightful father will be astute enough to spot what's going on here — that the boy is only making a fuss for the pure joy of seeing his sister get into trouble. Which is why the experienced, insightful father will sit the boy down and say, "Now, junior, let's be reasonable here, you haven't played with that toy for years, and I don't see what harm there is in your sister getting some enjoyment out of it."

The only problem is, few fathers have an opportunity to become experienced and insightful because there have been just so many games on television, one of which is on RIGHT NOW, for crying out loud.

So most fathers will handle the problem thusly:

"Young lady, you give that back to your brother this instant, do you hear me?"

"But, DAAAAAAAAAADDDDDDDD, he NEVER plays with this! He hasn't played with this for YEARS."

"Your brother tells me that Magnificently Mangled Donatello is his absolute, positively favorite toy in the whole world, and — Oh MAN, was that a touchdown?"

Clearly, children don't fight over toys because they actually want them. In fact, once children have their so-called cherished toys back, they will immediately discard them in favor of something better. They just don't want anyone else, particularly a sibling, to enjoy them. This is why battles often erupt over items of dubious value.

"That's MY dust bunny!"[1]

"Is not!"

"Is so!"

Campaigns of Terror

A child's day is divided roughly as follows:

Sleeping	10.0 hours
Eating	0.5 hours
Trying to induce cardiac arrest in brother or sister	13.5 hours

Nothing gives a child greater satisfaction than to be able to leap from behind a door, shout "Boooooo!" and provoke a terrified shriek from a sibling. And nothing motivates a child more to do this than to have been a recent victim.

Often you'll come upon your daughter standing noiselessly outside a closed bathroom door. From inside you can hear your son humming, attending to his business, oblivious to the fact that the

---

[1]More about dust bunnies in the chapter on low-maintenance pets.

final act he'll perform on this planet is using the last sheet of toilet paper without bothering to put a new roll on the holder.

His number has come up.

"What are you waiting around here for?" you say to your daughter. "We have TWO bathrooms."

And she puts her index finger to her lips, giving you the international children's sign for "Geez, Dad, I'm working undercover here, do you mind?"

You can then count on a series of five, distinct sounds:

1. Toilet flushing
2. Sink water running
3. Bathroom door unlatching
4. "BOOOOOOOOOOO!"
5. "AAAHHHHHHHHH!"

Often, more sophisticated techniques are employed. The plastic spider, for example.

Imitation insects show up so often on the dinner plates of young children that it's a wonder they haven't been listed among the basic food groups in the Canada Food Guide.

If your child, who normally disappears whenever it's his turn to set the table, suddenly takes an interest in helping take the plates into the dining room for the evening meal, alarms should go off.

Trouble is brewing if you hear the following: "I think it's time you started giving me more responsibility at supper time, and I'm ready to start assuming some right now, so why don't you just let me put those mashed potatoes on my sister's plate and mold them into something quite lovely?"

Chances are, however, that his sister is three steps ahead of him and will switch her plate with his when he goes back to the kitchen to refill his milk glass, which he has emptied in a 1.5-second gulp before taking his first bite.

Once he returns and finally bites into his own plastic spider, you can be grateful that it wasn't hidden in beets, which stain like the dickens when you try to wipe them off the wallpaper.

135

And then there are the attempts to terrify a baby brother, some of which are more diabolical than others.

One person, whom we shall call David for the purposes of this delicate story, since that is his real name, was nearly committed as a young child, following the actions of an older sister.

When she babysat him, she would turn off all the lights and leap out from behind doors and sofas. This was not so much a game, as it was a medical experiment to see whether a child's eyes can literally pop out of his head, just like in the cartoons.

Sometimes, and this is absolutely true, she'd bring over her friends and hide them strategically throughout the house. Wherever David went, he would encounter someone intent on, if not actually bringing his life to an end, at least inducing complete and total loss of bladder control.

The older sister knew right to the minute when the parents would return home. With about 30 seconds to go, she'd plant a butcher's knife in David's hand and then run screaming into the headlights of her parents' car as it pulled into the driveway.

"He's trying to kill me!" she'd shriek.

Just as David's mother and father were about to sign the papers to have him sent away for observation and oodles of shock therapy (something that David might actually have enjoyed), the parents of one of the other teenage terrorists spilled the beans about what was really going on.

Fortunately, David has suffered no lasting effects from his experiences, so long as you don't count prolonged whimpering when asked to open a closet door.

Helping Siblings Resolve Their Differences

When things get really out of control, when brothers and sisters are unable to settle their problems without the use of the G.I. Joe Nuclear Detonation Playset, it may be necessary for dad to step in.

Although pistols-at-dawn may be the solution you're leaning

toward, other, more civilized, approaches are recommended by child care experts.

Raise them in separate counties: This can get expensive, depending on how many children you have and how badly they need to be separated. But giving each child his or her own postal code can do wonders in keeping them from each other's throats.

If they fight, no dessert: To encourage kids to behave, tell them you're buying Neapolitan ice cream for a treat after dinner. But if there's any fighting through the day, dessert is off.

You'll be amazed at how well this works, right up until the time that the ice cream is being spooned into the bowls.

"She got more chocolate than I did!"

"Did not! And you hogged all the strawberry!"

"No!"

"Yes!"

"Hey! Who used up the last of the sprinkles?"

Santa doesn't like kids who fight: Telling your kids this sometimes works, but it has limited effectiveness in January and February, and is nearly useless with older kids, say 23 and up, who haven't found work yet and are still living at home.

Scream like a crazy person: It's not very often you find this kind of advice in parenting manuals, which is downright surprising, considering it's THE method of choice for mothers and fathers everywhere. And not just for solving sibling rivalry disputes.

When the kids have been chipping off each other all day, trading insults, whacking each other with their toys, and biting off earlobes, gather them together and, in as nurturing a way as possible, say:

"IF YOU DON'T STOP THIS FIGHTING I'M GOING TO STICK MY HEAD IN THE OVEN!"

Realizing that they would then be responsible for preparing their own dinner, most children will settle down at this point for at least four minutes.

19

Toys

(Or: How much will it cost you to keep the Barbie House building inspector in your pocket?)

Shortly after he concluded his research with canines, the brilliant behavioral scientist Pavlov (known to his buddies as "Professor Dog-Drool") turned his attention to written and spoken stimulus and parental response.

What he was seeking was a combination of rage, hopelessness, and frustration. Were there any phrases that could instantly bring about such feelings, all at the same time?

The answer was yes:

"Some assembly required"
"Batteries not included"
"Accessories sold separately"

We are, of course, talking about toys. "Batteries not included" and "Accessories sold separately" provoked equal expressions of rage and exasperation among parents. The first phrase, however, when encountered on the packaging of a child's new toy, provoked different reactions from mothers and fathers.

Mothers did not become agitated, nor did their heart rates begin to climb. The most typical response was a single word, invariably directed at the father: "Here."

Men, on the other hand, were often reduced to whimpering weasels. They were desolate — including architects and men who made their living as structural engineers and regular guys who can always figure out how to assemble a set of Ikea bookshelves without even looking at the instructions (which would be, let's face it, unmanly).

In fact, if you want to see a grown man cry, drop in on a father who's attempting, on Christmas Eve, in a bid to make his little girl (now fast asleep) the happiest little girl in the whole entire world on Christmas morning, to construct a Barbie House.

The two-storey Barbie House is, by modern-day toy standards, a relatively simple item to assemble. It consists of a molded plastic staircase, cardboard carpeting, 367 pink plastic girder pieces, 263 feet of wiring, 94 electrical outlets, a built-in vacuum system, track lighting, fully operational plumbing system with working bidet, completely equipped kitchen with (thank God) self-cleaning oven, documentation to prove that the dwelling is rent-controlled, and a complete set of striking unionized bricklayer action figures.

The father spreads all the pieces on the floor around him, pours himself a double Scotch, and begins by sorting pieces according to the 2,498-page instruction manual.

How hard could it be?

Several hours later, with two walls framed in an architectural style that could be described as "Frank Lloyd Wright's Freddy Guggenheim Period," there is a knock at the front door. Perhaps it is Santa himself, bringing a fully assembled version of the Barbie House.

No such luck.

It is a city building inspector wanting to know why such a project has been undertaken without first obtaining a municipal building permit.

This is, the dad is informed, the equivalent of putting a two-car garage onto the house, which the dad knows is positively ridiculous, because a new garage would have been much easier.

The inspector takes a look at what's been accomplished so far, slaps a stop-work order on it, and, while he's there, wants to know why no permit was ever obtained when all this wood panelling went up in the basement.

Ho ho ho.

Swimming Against the Gender Tide

Many parents are concerned about toys that may stereotype their children. Actually, many *mothers* are worried about this. Most fathers do not care, until their sons start playing with Betsy Wetsy, at which time they will supply their boys with as many stereotyped war and truck and gun and building and sports toys as they can find.

But there are some legitimate concerns here. Should girls who show a natural tendency to things mechanical be denied Lego and Meccano? And should boys who exhibit a sensitive side be forbidden to play "house," where they may pretend to feed and care for babies?[1]

Toy companies are well aware that it's time to gear toys that can be enjoyed by both sexes. That's why you'll soon be seeing some of the following on the shelves of your local mega toy store.

Easy-Bake Predators: Take care of these alien nasties once and for all. Just lock them into the Centauri IX Interstellar Microwave Oven (safe for children over the age of 43), set it on "Vaporize," and watch those suckers explode! Hours of fun! (Requires six DieHard car batteries, not included.)

Ninja Lamb Chop: See the Shari Lewis creation like you've never seen her before, jumping and chopping and beating the crap out of anyone who gets in her way.

---

[1]Does this deserve an answer?

Combat Barbie: The world's favorite doll is off to war! She comes complete with helmet, gas mask, and special high-heeled army boots (since that's the only kind that will fit Barbie's permanently deformed feet). A talking version ("Broke another nail on one of those darned grenade pins") is said to be in the works. (Includes designer fatigues, made exclusively for Barbie by Pierre Cardin.)

Ken the Riveter: Barbie's main squeeze keeps the home fires burning while she goes off to make the world safe for democracy. (Apron set sold separately.)

Polly's Pocket of Death: This popular line of toys, formerly aimed at girls and featuring miniature figures and their tiny play environments that fold up like a compact and fit into pockets, will now be getting lots of interest from boys. Just flip open the latest version to find Dr. Pollystein working away in her miniature lab, bringing roadkill back to life with jumper cables. (Comes with one dead raccoon figure; squirrel, rabbit, and porcupine sets also available.)

The Baby-Sitters Club in Mortal Kombat: A terrific new video game (Super NES and Sega), featuring Kristy and Claudia and Stacey and the rest of the gang from the bestselling series of books for girls. Watch them get revenge against parents who try to stiff them for the last hour of babysitting when they get home a little early. Extra points if you rip their heads off with the spine still attached.

Incontinent Robocop Action Figures: Oh sure, they rebuilt him into this magnificent crime-fighting man/machine, but what about bladder control? Did anyone ever give a thought to THAT? Girls who've enjoyed playing with dolls that wet, but hanker for something a little more adventurous, will love Robocop action figures that lose control of themselves after downing some futuristic "silicone beer." And the kids have to act fast to get him into some dry armor, before he completely short-circuits!

Pit Bull Plush Toys: Boys who think those 101 Dalmations are just a bit TOO cute will love this new line of stuffed dogs that gnaw your leg off when you hug them.

The Trip to the Toy Store

There's no use telling you not to make this trip.

It is inevitable that, as a father, one day you'll have to accompany your children to the neighborhood toy store — one of those gargantuan places that span more than one time zone, where employees at one end of the store are eating breakfast as the sun comes up and employees at the other end are having dinner by moonlight. It can be very stressful.

The main symptoms exhibited by a father about to embark on such a trip are cold sweats, shortness of breath, and a compulsion to destroy all charge cards before leaving the house.

Give your child the standard pre-toy store speech: "We are just going there to LOOK for some ideas for Christmas, not to BUY anything. The only thing we are buying today is a birthday gift for Timmy, whose party you are going to later today. Let me repeat: We are not buying ANYTHING today. Do you understand?"

"What if I bring my own money?"

"How much do you have?"

"Three dollars."

"Well, we'll see."

When you arrive at the toy store your child will race ahead, three precious dollars clutched in his fist, looking for something he can buy all on his own.

"How about this?" he asks, showing you a slot car set.

"Uh, that's $129."

He finds a castle construction set. "What about this?"

"That's $62.35, sport."

Then a model pickup truck kit.

"It's $22.50. Plus you need paints and glue."

He is starting to look pretty dejected by this point. He hands you a metal dump truck that beeps when you back it up.

"That's $39.95."

So now your child bursts into tears in the middle of the store, screaming: "YOU SAID I COULD GET SOMETHING BUT THERE ISN'T ANYTHING I CAN GET!"

And all the other parents will stop and look at you and they will be thinking: "And he calls himself a father, promising his kid something and then reneging."

"Okay, okay, okay," you say, trying to calm your child down. "Maybe, *maybe*, if Daddy just added a little something to your $3, maybe *then* you'd still be able to buy something. Just . . . just stop crying."

Have a good story for your wife when the two of you arrive home with Dr. Disgusting's Decapitation Playset, which your son paid for with his own $3, and only another $66.99 from you.

Tell her you put it on the GM MasterCard, so now you'll get points toward a Cavalier.

Educational Toys

Should toys be more than just fun? Should they also teach kids something? Or is combining play with education a major bummer?

Look at how the Sesame Street toys have helped children learn to read and count. Fisher-Price toys help young minds solve problems.

But the fact is, valuable lessons can be learned from almost any kind of toy. Often, they are lessons for you, the PARENT. For example:

1. The grandparents must have it in for you, otherwise why would they have bought Junior a toy car with a friction motor in it that sounds like 12 cats being sucked into a jet turbine?
2. Plastic must be one of the world's most valuable resources. How else could they charge $49.87 for the Nuclear Tumor Turtle Bomb Shelter Playset, which lasted exactly 2.3 minutes before collapsing into a thousand pieces.
3. The death penalty is not cruel and unusual punishment, at least not for the people who produce toy commercials.

4. Certain toys can provoke violent behavior in children. After your two children fight over who can sleep with the stuffed Mufasa from *The Lion King*, you urge the toy standards council to pull it off the shelves everywhere.

5. Trucks that can transform themselves into robots and then back again into trucks is the stupidest idea you've ever heard of, and you can't for the life of you figure out why you didn't come up with it first.

6. You really CAN get into trouble if you run into a bank carrying a Nerf bow and arrow.

7. "I had to stay home and untangle my daughter's Slinky" is not, in most places of employment, an acceptable excuse for taking the day off work.

8. Migraine sufferers should never, ever, give their children musical instruments of any kind. Especially drums.

9. If you're really proud that your child is able to make a fully operating electric chair with his Meccano set, think again.

10. Mr. Potato Head does not work with Pringles.

20

Taking Kids Shopping

(Or: Have you completely lost your mind?)

Let's kick things off with another one of our short quizzes.

In each of the three following questions, select which item you are more likely to know.

1. a) your child's shoe size.
   b) which one is Beavis and which one is Butt-head.
2. a) your child's pant size.
   b) the number of consecutive baseball games Cal Ripken Jr. had to play to break Lou Gehrig's record.
3. a) your child's shirt size.
   b) the titles of all the episodes from the original *Star Trek*, in order, with the names of the major guest stars.

How embarrassed, exactly, do you feel right now, on a scale of 1 to 10?

Chances are, even if you were unable to answer any of the

questions about the size of clothes your child takes, you aren't embarrassed in the slightest, but you're kicking yourself because you thought "The Gamesters of Triskelion" came before "The City on the Edge of Forever."

No matter how hard dads try to remember such seemingly vital information as the sizes their children wear, it just doesn't do any good. The male brain is incapable of storing such information. There is, to put it simply, no room at the inn.

It has always been this way. Some of the earliest studies from around the time of World War II were conducted on soldiers working in the espionage branches of the military.

They could, for example, remember the complicated decoding process to turn the phrase "Your Momma looks like Rosie the Riveter" into "the Allied Forces land at dawn," but were unable to recall that their son might take a size 6 in Keds.

One would like to say that this is the kind of information mothers are better at storing and recalling, but it's perilous to suggest such a thing in the current political climate. To even hint at this would be to suggest that somehow it's BENEATH men to concern themselves with such matters. (Although, if you were to turn things around, and ask your spouse to whip over to Canadian Tire and pick up some lag bolts, you'd get a look that indicated she thought you were operating with a few bolts loose yourself.)

It's not beneath men at all to know such things. But to argue the point on this level is a waste of time. The simplest way for you as a father to remain uninvolved in the purchase of your children's clothes, and the safest politically, is to say you are too stupid.

Even if you do not believe this to be the case,[1] it will be accepted without argument by your spouse.

But as much as fathers want nothing to do with shopping for clothes for their children, there are times that they must make the effort; if not in actually selecting the items, then in standing outside

---

[1]And you would be wrong.

146

the change room offering opinions once their kids step out to model something new.

Believe it or not, your spouse actually wants your input, or at least she will until you offer it.

Wife: (as child comes out of change room) Okay, turn around, let's have a look at you. *(To husband)* What do you think of those?
Husband: (shrugging) Well, they seem a little short in the leg.
Wife: They're shorts.
Husband: Then I guess they're okay.

Often, a father must have some firm criteria on which to base his choices for his kids. Are the child's clothes TOO trendy, or so radical that he'll tire of wearing them after the first time? Are they made of the finest quality fabrics?

Let's suppose you are presented with a child trying on a red plaid top, and then a blue striped top.

Wife: Which do you like better?
Husband: How much is the red top?
Wife: $15.99.
Husband: How much is the blue top?
Wife: $16.99.
Husband: I think that red one is really sharp.

And while we're on the topic of price, be prepared to explain to your children why it is not as important as they think for them to have brand-name goods. Point out to your kids that there's no good reason to spend $79 on a pair of Reeboks when you can get an excellent no-name shoe for $29, unless they won't be able to sleep that night knowing that another NBA star is going to bed without his fifth Ferrari.

Tell them that when you were growing up you managed quite nicely, thank you very much, without Doc Marten boots, Nikes, Laura Ashley dresses (well, that goes without saying), Ralph Lauren rugby shirts, and pre-ripped Calvin Klein jeans. Tell them that when you were growing up, if it kept you covered, and it said K Mart on it, it was good enough for you. Tell them that it doesn't matter what their friends are wearing, it's what's inside that counts, and there's no reason for them to become slaves to the whims of advertisers.

After you've finished this speech, and bought them their Bi-Way jeans and Wal-Mart sneakers, take them home weeping and wailing in your Eddie Bauer version Ford Explorer, putting the pedal to the metal with your new Bass Weejuns, being careful not to scratch your wife's BMW 318i when you pull into the driveway.

When Shopping Gets Boring

Generally speaking, if it's not a toy store they're in, children will become bored very quickly when shopping with grown-ups. And when they become bored, they start whining, making it very difficult for you to get those important things on your list.

The smart father has to come up with ways to keep his children entertained just long enough that he can get his business done. The key is finding a game for them to play, and that depends largely on what kind of store you're in.

For example, at a plumbing store, tell your kids to go find a "ball-cock assembly." They will think it's something dirty, and tear the place apart until they find one.

At the lawn and garden center, tell them to keep sniffing all the flowers until they find the one that smells just like their Aunt Thelma, the longshoreman.

At the bookstore, tell them that you THINK this is the place where, in the middle of just one of the books in the store, they hide a $1,000 bill.

If you're looking for new wallpaper, hand them a few sample books and tell them they're allowed, JUST THIS ONCE, to flip through them, as long as they promise NOT to look at any of the pictures of naked people.

"We promise! We promise!" they will reply.

These are all, admittedly, pretty sneaky things to do. But they beat the alternative, which is to turn into a screaming lunatic in the middle of a crowded Home Depot, demanding that your children stop whining and punching each other long enough for you to select a new weed whacker. The chances, however, of your being allowed to purchase something like a weed whacker after putting on a public display that seems to suggest, at the very least, that you are the president of the local Charles Manson fan club, are not very good. Especially after the store security team calls 911 and subdues you with a miniature fire extinguisher, the kind that can put out kitchen grease fires, which you've been meaning to buy for some time now.

All of this can bring great shame upon your family, because without a weed whacker the edges of your driveway, sidewalk, and new patio will become unsightly with countless blades of uncut grass.

If there's a greater social embarrassment for a suburban-type dad, we don't know what it is.

At the Grocery Store

We've heard a lot about how technology is going to revolutionize the grocery shopping experience.

Someday, a computer will memorize your purchases from your last visit to the store. Then the next time you're pushing your computerized cart, it will alert you, with its annoying, digitized voice, every time you pass something that's appeared on your list before.

"Whoa!" it will say. "You just went past the Pop-Tarts! You bought the Strawberry Frosted on August 19, September 12, and October 1. We can see that a healthy diet is a real priority in your house!"

But those of us with young children are already on the cutting edge. We don't need shopping lists or computers to tell us what to buy.

"Oh! OH! DAD! Cap'n Crunch!"

"DAD! Don't forget the Fruit Roll-ups! Mom ALWAYS gets us some Fruit Roll-ups!"

"Wieners! We've got to have WIENERS!"

"You went right past the cupcakes! I'm calling the child welfare people!"

"Stop the cart! STOP THE CART! Gushers! We've GOT to have Gushers!"

"Hey! Hey! That's the cereal I saw on TV! The one with the Batmobile on the box!"

You point out that the Batmobile is on a box of Healthy Nut 'N'Crunchy Dirt and Soil Flakes, which your child has actually tried before, when Ren and Stimpy were on the cover. It was a memorable breakfast experience, mainly because your child expectorated with such force that he knocked your glasses off.

"But it's got the Batmobile on it!"

The only trouble with relying on a child as your shopping list is that this means your youngster is, in effect, planning your week's menus.

Make up your own list, because if it were left to a child to plan the week's meals, they would look something like the following.

	Sunday	Monday	Tuesday	Wednesday	Thursday	Friday	Saturday
B R E A K F A S T	cherry Danish	Frosted Flakes mixed with Count Chocula and fudge sauce, Freshie	leftover frozen pizza, Pepsi, Nerd candies	Mars bar with grape jelly	nine Oreos dipped in milk (the milk makes this the week's most healthy meal)	pure Nestlé Quik powder on toast	since it's the weekend, time for some Lucky Charms
L U N C H	hot dogs	gum on a bun	peanut butter on cake	strange round meat pieces in a plastic tray, with cracker	swap whatever you have for what your class-mate's got	chicken nuggets you've been hiding under your bed since Easter	frozen pizza, frozen fries, right out of the freezer
D I N N E R	hound parents to go out for hot dogs, since you haven't had them since lunch	hound parents to go out for fried chicken with special 12-inch thick batter, which can also be used for asphalt repair	hound parents to go out for a Big Mac and shakes and hot apple pies, because fruit is vital for healthy diets	hound parents to go out for a Whopper (for a bit of variety) to get special "The Mask" part VI cup	hound parents to go out for cheese-filled crusty pizza because you get a cheap plastic toy after	hound parents to go out for tacos made with 100% all natural rodent parts	hound parents to go to grand-parents where they can get some REAL food for a change

21

Discipline

(Or: How to completely lose control, scream like a deranged, parental lunatic, but in a NURTURING way)

The proper disciplining of children is one of the most difficult tasks a father will face. And after reading what the experts have to say, talking to other parents, and learning through plain old trial and error, many dads will conclude that if there's to be any hope of keeping the children in line, their wives are simply going to have to seize control of the situation.

The odd father, however, will decide to involve himself in the process, and this is where real, practical advice can be so useful. We're only sorry we aren't able to provide any.

To Spank or Not to Spank

When our generation was young, no one gave much thought to whether spanking was an appropriate, effective method of punishment.

Today, before we spank, we ask ourselves the following questions.

1. If I spank my child, is it just teaching him to use violence to resolve conflicts?
2. Is the spanking really a deterrent, or just a way to vent my own anger?
3. What are the wider social implications of a society that hits its young?

But in the old days, the three questions that concerned parents had to weigh were:
1. Back of hand?
2. Strap?
3. Hickory switch?

Realizing that in the '90s they just can't go around hitting their kids, many parents have opted for alternative methods of discipline. But to deal with their unresolved anger, they've taken to kicking their dogs. (This, however, has also taken on something of a negative context, considering that society's outrage at attacks on cute and furry animals generally outstrips its concern for children.)

If you're walking through the mall and whack your child on the side of the head, people will frown and mutter under their breath, but they won't actually DO anything. But if you're walking the dog down the street and do the same thing to Rover, several anonymous calls will be made to the local animal rights league, which will take time out from putting glue in the locks of hamburger outlets to surround you with its special tactical team, strip you naked, and have you tarred and feathered (synthetic feathers only; no actual chickens were plucked for their production).

Anyway, let's take a look at some spanking alternatives.

Send Your Child to His Room

This is a very effective way of letting your child know that his behavior's unacceptable; isolating him sends a message that he does not deserve to be around other members of his family. He will just have to entertain himself for awhile with nothing more than

153

his ghetto blaster, 135 CDs, personal computer and CD-ROM loaded with Doom and Myst and other up-to-date hi-tech games, private phone line, all 5,873 R. L. Stine horror novels, and the March issue of *Playboy*, which has been hidden under his mattress for several weeks now.

One of the drawbacks to this disciplining method is that, once you've ordered him to his room, and a sense of calm and order descends on the rest of the household, you may forget you sent him there. Several hours later, you will say to your wife: "Have you seen Waldo? Where's Waldo?"

Calling for him will be pointless, because he'll be listening, under headphones that have been set to "Complete Eardrum Destruction," to the latest recording from Totally Regurgitated Lamb Vomit.

In a panic, you and your spouse will get in the car and cruise the neighborhood, knocking on people's doors, running into the local comic book and music shops, deciding finally that the only thing to do is go back home and call the authorities, who, it turns out, are already there, having been called by your son who went into a similar, complete panic when he discovered he'd been left home alone.

To ensure that you don't get cited for some parental violation of the criminal code, be sure to point out to the police officer that, as a taxpayer, you PAY HIS SALARY, and he better remember WHO HE'S TALKING TO.

Cops really like that.

TALK to Your Child

This has become a modern-day favorite, and is highly recommended by child psychologists. To see how effective it is, examine the following transcript.

Father: Now, son, you know what you did was wrong, don't you?
Damien: Grrrrrrr.
Father: You know your mother and I have TOLD you not to trap the mailman and perform your little experiments on him.

Damien: (burning "666" into the dining room table with his new KidPro Woodburning Kit) The power of evil is upon you.

Father: And that business with your sister's pet rabbit, you know that was wrong. Now, I will admit, you prepared it beautifully, the spices were excellent, but you could just as easily have used chicken.

Damien: (turning his head around 360 degrees and spewing green slime all over the walls and furniture) Don't for a moment think that anyone will escape alive. You cannot defeat me.

Father: Well, there, I hope this little chat helped. Now run along and play!

Withdrawing Privileges

Let's suppose your daughter has changed the Ds on her Grade 5 report card into Bs, a trick you used to pull with some creative pencil work when you were a kid, but which is a MAJOR accomplishment in the '90s, since all the report cards are computerized, indicating that your little princess has cracked the school board's computer system and is well on her way to infiltrating the Pentagon.

You can't allow this kind of thing to go unpunished, so you decide that next week, when the family is scheduled to go to Disney World, the Universal Studios theme park, Busch Gardens, and Clearwater Beach, she'll have to bring along her OLD pail and shovel, instead of getting a new one once you get down there.

There will be a lot of whining and moaning and complaining about this, but sometimes you just have to get TOUGH.

The Importance of Consistency and Following Through

This, above all, is the key to disciplining your youngster. There must be consequences for misbehaving, and they must be consistent.

When you tell a child to stop doing something that is wrong, dangerous, and/or annoying, he must know that you mean business. That's why we recommend our world-renowned, positively

155

foolproof, 12-Step Warning System for Ankle Biters.

At the first sign of trouble, say the following 12 things to your child, usually allowing anywhere from 10 minutes to several hours between each step.

☆

The 12-Step Warning System

1. "Stop that."
2. "I thought I told you to stop that."
3. "You stop that right NOW."
4. "Billllllyyyyyy!" (or whatever)
5. "If you don't stop that right now, there's going to be trouble, young man."
6. "I. DO. NOT. LIKE. WHAT. I'M. SEEING."
7. "Billllllyyyyyy!" (or whatever)
8. "All right, buster, I'm going to start counting. One . . . two . . . three . . ."
9. "Seventy-two . . . seventy-three . . ."
10. "Well I think I've had just about enough of that!"
11. "Billllllyyyyyy!" (or whatever)
12. "Okay, that's it, I'm telling your mother."

Some of you may wish to bypass a few of these steps, and adopt a different approach, more in line with the method that was probably utilized by your own father. This technique often involves special voice training, not unlike what professional singers and yodelers undertake, because it consists, primarily, of . . .

Yelling

Just as many foolish people embark on an exercise regime, say jogging or weight lifting, without first consulting a doctor, or even doing something as simple as a warm-up, far too many fathers are screaming their heads off without adequate training.

The vocal cords are a delicate instrument and should be treated accordingly. You shouldn't embark on a lifetime of yelling at your children without first making sure you are up to it.

Try this simple exercise next time you're out driving by yourself. As loud as you can, scream: "WHAT'S THE MATTER, YOUR CAR STUCK IN NEUTRAL, BOZO???!!!"

Then ask yourself, how did that feel? Did you immediately get a hoarseness in the back of your throat? Did your eyes bug out uncomfortably? If you wear contacts, did they pop off? If you're a tad overweight, did your sudden intake of breath before screaming suddenly turn your shirt buttons into projectiles that went slamming into the windshield?

If the answer to any of these questions is yes, yelling may not be the most sensible disciplinary tool in your household. Nothing undermines your attempts to impose order on obstreperous youngsters more than your toupee flying off, your face turning blue, and your pants falling down.

Never-Fail Disciplinary Phrases

Some of the things your parents said to you when they were angry were pretty effective back in the '50s and '60s, but today, not only do they sound dated, but they also fail to live up to the politically correct standards we've set for ourselves.

Today, even when we are ticked with our kids and let them know it, we want to do it in a way that will be firm but *nurturing.*

Sure, it can be unsettling when your child forgets to turn off the tap in the downstairs bathroom and no one notices until you find the rec room sofa floating three feet off the floor, but hurling insults and offering unconstructive criticism at a time like this can be very damaging to the child's self-esteem.

You don't want to inflict any lifelong scars, and then have to fork out thousands for therapy sessions — you're going to need that money to dry out your basement.

Below you'll find some '90s alternatives to help you out.

What your parents used to say to you	What you say to your own kids in the '90s
"If all your friends wanted to jump off a cliff, would you do it, too?"	"If all your friends decided to use virus-infected software and wear their shirts tucked in and their ballcaps with the visor forward and regular shoes WITH NO BRAND NAMES ON THEM, would you do it, too?"
"Because I said so, that's why."	"As one of the two primary care-givers in this family, I certainly appreciate your input and VALUE your opinion, but I feel things would run more smoothly if my instructions were followed with a minimum of questioning, you little (unintelligible)."
"No!"	"Why don't we sit down and discuss the pros and cons of the situation and I'm sure that, on your own, you'll see that I've made the right decision for you, and if you think differently, we'll tell the Tooth Fairy we have an unlisted address."
"Hit your sister again and I'll kick your backside so hard they'll be picking you up off the street in Temiskaming."	"I think you should get in touch with the source of your anger, before I get in touch with the source of mine, big time."

22

Wisdom

(Or: "Step aside, son, and let Poppa show you how to get to Level 4")

As a father, you will be expected to be wise.

Do not panic.

Your children will automatically assume that you are wise. Think back to your own father, and how, even to this day, you cherish the words of wisdom that he passed on to you when you were just a young boy.

Things like: "Always hold the cafeteria tray by the edge closest to you so you don't get your fingers pinched by the next person."

Or: "Always eat your greens, unless it happens to be meat, in which case give it a pass."

Or: "Contrary to what you may have heard, women are not attracted to men who pick their feet in public."

These are the kinds of morsels of genuine insight that have shaped us into the kinds of men we are today. We owe it to our sons and daughters to pass on to them equally helpful tips to guide them through their lives. But first we need a bit of background.

The Great Philosophers

Learning from the greatest thinkers in our history is a super way to make yourself much wiser than you already may be.

So who do you immediately think of, then, when the words "great thinker" are tossed out?

Well, chances are if you're like most modern males, the name Ben (Obi-Wan) Kenobi comes to mind. Here was a guy who not only looked like Alec Guinness (one of the wisest actors of the 20th century), but also knew everything about the galaxy and how to coin nifty phrases like "May the Force be with you."

Coming a close second would have to be his associate Yoda, who looked like a cross between Einstein and E.T. and could teach people to move things with their minds, which is a terrific skill to master if you're stuck under the kitchen sink trying to hold two pipes together and realize you've left your monkey wrench in the toolbox, ten feet away.

Finally, there's Mr. Spock, of *Star Trek* fame, who's known for the extremely wise "The needs of the many outweigh the needs of the few," a handy thing to quote on a Sunday afternoon when you and your three buddies want to watch the game and your two kids want to watch the *Pocahontas* video for the 145th time.

You may have other favorite sources of inspirational wisdom: Splinter, the philosopher rat of the *Teenage Mutant Ninja Turtles*; the *Karate Kid* movies; David Carradine in *Kung Fu*; those touching little speeches Andy gave to Opie. So it may come as a surprise to many of you dads out there that most of the world's great philosophers were not, strictly speaking, fictional. Some of the people whose catchy sayings are being repeated all the time by friends and associates whom we would categorize as "smartypants" actually existed at one time.

To make an impression on your children, you should start reading the works of these famous philosophers. But most of these know-it-alls tended to use old-fashioned language to get their ideas across, which isn't surprising when you consider that there have been no great thinkers since the invention of television. So their works can be tough sledding for fathers whose reading is limited primarily to crossword puzzles and John Grisham novels.

To see whether you're up to the task, read the following quotation from Confucius, and then pick the answer you think comes closest to its meaning:

"When you know a thing, to hold that you know it; and when you do not know a thing, to allow that you do not know it — that's knowledge."

This means:

a) "Huh?"
b) "Could you repeat the question?"
c) "Life is like a box of chocolates."

If you picked (c), you know a phrase spoken by a true genius when you hear it.

So dust off some of those classics that are at the back of your bookshelf and dig in for those nuggets of braininess, which can work wonders when dealing with your children.

For example, for the child complaining that you're three weeks behind in her allowance, merely quote Sophocles: "Wisdom outweighs our wealth." (You might as well try it on your child, since it's NOT going to work with your landlord.) What kid's going to want money when she knows a snappy comeback is worth so much more?

Or how about when Sophocles says, "Sons are the anchors of a mother's life." Any fool can tell that what he's really saying is: "Go ask your Ma."[1]

Here are a few others you can jot down.

Plato: "You are young, my son, and, as the years go by, time will change and even reverse many of your present opinions. Refrain

---

[1] It should be noted, for no particular reason, that Christopher Columbus, noted explorer, discoverer of the New World and all around helpful guy who delayed his expedition until 1492 just so that it could rhyme with "ocean blue," is believed to be the very first person to have used the phrase: "Are we there yet?"

therefore awhile from setting yourself up as a judge of the highest matters."

Translation: "Shut up."

Aristotle: "We should behave to our friends as we would wish our friends to behave to us."

Translation: "Maybe if you hadn't put glue in Jimmy's pockets he wouldn't have filled your shorts with raspberry Jell-O."

Aesop: "The gods help them that help themselves."

Translation: "You're on your own, kid."

Confucius: "Is virtue a thing remote? I wish to be virtuous, and lo! virtue is at hand."

Translation: "Give me the clicker."

Homer: "Whoever obeys the gods, to him they particularly listen."

Translation: "You promise not to tell Mom it was me who backed the car into her garden and I'll see that you get your Rollerblades."

Homer Simpson: "Doh!"

Translation: "Doh!"

Don't ever bother, however, to quote Socrates' last words: "Crito, I owe a cock to Asclepius; will you remember to pay the debt?" Whatever meaning this holds will be lost on children, who will collapse in immense fits of giggling, in much the same manner as when you ask them which part of the chicken they would like, and they squeal hysterically: "Breast!"

How to Look Wise

You can effect an extremely wise manner not so much by what you do, but by what you DON'T do.

The list of things you should not do includes:

- breathing with your mouth open and letting flies get in there
- sticking the hose down your pants when checking the air pressure in your tires at the gas station

- showing up at parent-teacher night all ready to go fly-fishing, including wearing hip waders
- wearing socks with sandals
- playing your Neil Diamond records loud enough for the neighbors to hear
- wearing a rug that looks more like a comatose bichon frise
- along with your wife, wearing shirts that say "I'm Stupid" and "I'm with Stupid"; it makes no difference who's wearing which shirt
- calling your kids' favorite bands "Nervosa" and "R.P.M."

But there are still a few things you CAN do to make yourself appear like a fountain of wisdom. Chief among these is adopting the look of a university professor.

This look entails:

- tweed jacket with elbow patches
- pipe
- some kind of facial hair, either a moustache or beard or both
- wandering the mall parking lot for several hours trying to find your Volvo, then remembering you do not own a car
- knowing all the good Agamemnon knock-knock jokes
- having 20-year-old female students, who swoon when you go by, find you attractive for no apparent reason whatsoever, except that you put a nice spin on the word "syllabus"

This approach may not work as well, however, with youngsters totally unacquainted with the postsecondary environment. You're better off selecting a look with which they are more familiar.

Try "Do-Bee," that buzzing bug of knowledge from the *Romper Room* television show. Do-Bee not only knows all the bike safety rules and how to cross the street without becoming windshield pizza, he also knows how to screw in a lightbulb without zapping his stinger off.

Should an adult happen to find you so costumed, explain that it's your own way of paying homage to the late, great John Belushi.

Your Test

Okay, it's time to test what you've learned so far. In the following scenario, choose the words of advice for your child that strike you as being the most wise:

Your son has spent the last 30 minutes in total frustration in front of the television, video game controller in hand, trying to get Mucous Membrane Max out of the Throat of Doom and into the next level, River of Radioactive Phlegm, but can't find the way.

What should you say to him?

a) "When I was a boy, we didn't have video games. We played baseball and tag and hide-and-seek, and got some fresh air, and didn't sit around all day in front of a box letting our eyes go square. 'Interactive' was not the word of the day, it was 'interaction,' and it was carried out with real, live, friends."

b) "Look behind the Adam's Apple and you'll find a special grappling hook that will get you there. At least it worked for me last night when I was playing it."

If you picked (b), you are one terrific, involved dad.

However, don't expect that your wisdom will always sink in. There may come times when the message is sound, but the kids, like a 20-year-old Zenith with a busted antenna, aren't picking up the signal.

For example:

"It was so STUPID!" your daughter says. "We had half an hour to play Capture the Flag, but no one could decide who'd be on which team, and then Rachel said she wanted to be on MY team but she was already on the OTHER team and she said she wouldn't play, so we said she could switch, but then Jessica DIDN'T want to be on my team so she said she was going to go home, and before you knew it, all the time was up and we never even got to play at all!"

"You know," you say, positively reeking of wisdom, "your situation puts me in mind of the story of the donkey and the two bales of straw."

"What's that story?"

"Well, once upon a time, there was a very hungry donkey, and he couldn't decide which bale of straw to eat first, and because he was paralyzed by indecision, he ultimately starved to death."

"Wow! If I was really hungry and I had two subs in front of me, and they were both assorteds, with mayo and tomatoes, I wonder which I would eat first? OH! If one was a 6-inch, and the other was a 12-inch, I think I'd start with the 6-inch, because it — NO! I'd eat the BIG one first, but NOT if they accidentally got black olives on it, but —"

"I'm not really sure that this is the point —"

"Are you hungry?"

23

Keeping the Marriage Alive

(Or: "Oh Ruuuuby, I won't take your calf to town")

Way back in Chapter 5, where we discussed Sex, we concluded that just because you and your spouse are busy raising a family doesn't mean that you can't still have a rich and rewarding sex life.

Of course, as you know by now, we were just kidding about that.

The only way you can be absolutely certain of maintaining the kind of wild and frenetic sex you had as newlyweds is if, instead of children, you decide to raise cactus.

But we'd still like to make the point that having children doesn't mean you give up on the relationship. You must not take your mate for granted. You must remember, every single day, to show her that you still love her, even if you have been too busy getting strained peas out of the carpet to actually tell her.

Many North American men got a wake-up call about the importance of not taking their wives for granted from that book and movie sensation *The Bridges of Madison County*, which has been on the best-seller list since Mackenzie King made his dog finance minister.

166

In case you are the only man left in North America who does not know what that story's about (in other words, you have been on the Jupiter Mission), it concerns an Iowa farmer's wife who, while her husband and kids are away for four days showing off a prize calf at a fair, has a passionate affair with a photographer from *National Geographic* magazine.

(If you are a guy and are familiar with this story it's not because you read the book. There's not a man around who actually read this book, except perhaps for some male book reviewers, and even most of them had their wives or girlfriends read it and just tell them what it was about. Or else they got the *Cole's Notes*. Men only agreed to go to the movie because Clint "Dirty Harry" Eastwood was in it, and there was always the hope that sooner or later he'd blow someone away, even if it was only a cow.)

Anyway, there's a key scene early on in this movie, where Meryl Streep, who plays the farmer's wife, makes dinner for her husband and children, who chow it down like they are expecting a flock of rabid sheep to bust in at any moment and take it from them. All without so much as a "thank you" or "great meal" or "pass the potatoes" or "golly, Ma, you're so quiet, are you perhaps feeling a mid-life angst that's being exacerbated by passions that have gone untapped?"

So off they go to the fair with their calf, and in walks Eastwood, looking for directions to those covered bridges and saying, "make my dinner." Before you can say "F-stop," the two of them are dancing across the linoleum and into the sack.

Lots of men in the audience, after making several trips back to the candy counter to load up on napkins for their sobbing wives, made mental notes about how to conduct themselves after seeing this movie.

These included:

1. Never move to Iowa.
2. Don't take your calf to any out-of-town shows. Mail a picture.
3. Cancel your *National Geographic* subscription.

Some men, incredibly, felt that there was even MORE work to be done to keep their marriages fresh and vibrant. They vowed to be more attentive, more sensitive, better at remembering special occasions, but stopped short of putting down the toilet seat.

Special Occasions

When you mention the words "special occasions" to dads, they immediately assume you're referring to Super Bowl Sunday, the launch date of the latest Microsoft computer operating system, or the 60th anniversary of the creation of Batman.

But there are other dates that fathers who do not wish to have their lungs ripped out would be wise to remember. Let's review them here.

Valentine's Day

This is the one named for St. Valentine, the inventor of the Hallmark card.

Valentine's Day is on February 14, even on leap years, and there are plenty of clues that it's coming. Chief among these is the heart symbol.

All these years you may have been thinking, as you strolled through the mall and saw all the card shops with heart decorations, and flower shops with heart decorations, and lingerie shops with heart decorations, that February was Cholesterol Awareness Month.

Give your head a shake. This is the month of Love. Of Romance. Of Roses and Cupids and Chocolates. And, most important of all, Husband Self-Preservation. There is no excuse for forgetting Valentine's Day.

First of all, buy your wife a card that professes your love for her. Be careful with humorous cards. You may think your wife enjoys a good joke as much as the next person, but she is unlikely to enjoy the witty thinking that went into: "Happy Valentine's Day, Dear, There's More of You to Love Every Day."

And don't forget flowers. Make sure you buy them from a reputable florist, and don't bother looking for bargains here. Although you may be tempted by the roadside flower vendor selling a dozen roses for $4.99, your reputation may suffer if, upon opening them at home, your wife finds them being devoured by Bolivian Rose Beetles the size of Chihuahuas.

Anniversaries

These are much trickier. Seeing as how the rest of the world is not aware of the date you and your wife took your vows, you can't expect major retail chains to undertake promotions that will jog your memory.

For example, it is unlikely, a week before your anniversary, that you'll open the paper to a full-page Sears ad that says: "Sid and Beth Celebrate 15 Years! See What We Have To Offer!"

If you're lucky, you have a wife who will drop subtle hints, like "You better not forget our anniversary, you knob" while making ominous pulsing noises with the food processor.

But your spouse MAY be waiting to see if you'll remember this important date all on your own.

Here's a helpful hint on how to do just that.

Let's say that the day you first promised to love, honor, and help with the vacuuming was June 15. There were 300 people there, your young bride looked positively radiant, you danced into the night, and, aside from your cousin Melvin throwing up on the cake, everything went great.

Now all you have to do is remember something ELSE that happened on or about that day that really meant a lot to you.

June 15, for example, might have been the day in 1978 when you changed the oil, on your own, for the very first time, in your 1969 Dodge Charger. This was your first car, and being able to look after it and service it yourself was very important to you. At the time, you kept a meticulous record of all maintenance.

June 11: "Washed and vacuumed Charger."

June 13: "Polished the jack."
June 14: "Armor-Alled dash for first time! Boy, it looks so shiny!"
June 15: "Changed the oil! With no help from Daddy!"

So now, each year as June 15 oil-change celebrations approach, you have to find a way to link, in your mind, that event with your wedding day. Through word association, find something common to both these events.

Let's see. There's oil and procession, and pan and cake, and change and veil, and — *WHOA!*

You've got it. The word is: Dipstick.

Not only does a dipstick tell you when you need to add oil, but it's been your father-in-law's favorite name for you from the moment your wife-to-be first introduced the two of you.

Birthdays

This is another tough one, since you also can't count on the stores to advertise it. The best thing to do is always keep your spouse's driver's license, which shows her birth date, in YOUR wallet, and every time you're in there for something, take a glance at it. One day, you're going to get lucky, and everyone's going to be happy.

This may lead to the odd moment of inconvenience for your wife, but a few days in the clinker for driving without a license is a small price to pay for marital tranquility.

Mother's Day

Unlike the previous occasions, the only way your wife is entitled to be recognized on this day is if the two of you have actually produced children.

If you happen to let this date get by without doing anything special for your significant other, you can hang it on the kids.

Surely, it's up to THEM to remember. She's THEIR mother. It's simply not your responsibility.

Going to the Movies

This is a great way to spend an evening with your wife. Just hire a sitter and away you go.

And to show you are a sensitive, '90s kind of dad, don't object to going to the occasional "chick flick."

Now "chick flick" is a derisive term some dads use to describe movies that are assumed to be of more interest to women than to men, as opposed to "doofus flicks," which are the kinds of pictures dads want to go see. The latter pose such thought-provoking questions as: Whose head could better withstand having a tractor trailer drive over it — Sylvester Stallone's or Jean-Claude Van Damme's?[1]

A perfect example of the "chick flick" is the aforementioned *The Bridges of Madison County*. Here are some tips to help you spot what is likely a "chick flick":

1. No names of weapons in the title.
2. The TV ads hype it with blurbs like, "This year's *Trip to Bountiful*."
3. Has women like Olympia Dukakis, Shirley MacLaine, or Kathy Bates in it.
4. No references to photon torpedoes.
5. When there's a shot of a car going around the corner, the hubcaps don't fly off.
6. When the final credits start to roll, most women in the audience will sound as though they are suffering from a nearly terminal ragweed allergy.

This is a good time to show that, despite being a lover of "doofus flicks," you do have a tender side. Comfort your wife, slip your arm around her shoulder as she's dabbing her tears, and, as the lights come up, say something like: "I feel like I could really strap on the ol' feedbag. How about you?"

What many people don't know is that an incredible number of movies intended for a primarily female audience nearly became guy movies in the early stages of production. But then somebody (who was not a man) said, "Hey, we're already doing *Die Really Really Hard*, so why don't we branch out a bit?"

The following chart provides some background.

---

[1]Stallone. It might be incredibly messy, but there would be no actual damage done.

Chick flicks that were originally doofus flicks

Final Title	Original Title
Waiting to Exhale	Waiting to Expunge
Sleepless in Seattle	Headless in Seattle
Muriel's Wedding	Muriel's Weed-Eater
Terms of Endearment	Terms of Surrender
Bridges of Madison County	Satanic Scarecrows of Madison County
While You Were Sleeping	While You Were Loading Your Howitzer

Going Out for Dinner

An evening in a charming restaurant, without the kids, is a great way to show the mother of your children that you not only still care about her, but also remain the sophisticated, debonair gent she married years ago.

Demonstrate your worldliness in dealing with your waiter or waitress:

"Yes, in fact, I WILL have fries with that."

Tell your wife that you've chosen this restaurant because it's quiet and romantic and reminds you of the place you used to take her when you were courting and wild with young love. Hide the coupon that gives you a second entree (of equal or lesser value) for free.

Finally, recalling the eating habits of Meryl Streep's husband in that infamous movie, do not bolt your food down as though it's an Olympic event. Chew your food carefully, and make conversation between bites. Get to know your wife all over again. Find out what makes her tick by posing the occasional interesting question, like:

"You wouldn't be upset, would you, if I said I have no interest in ever raising cattle?"

24

Homework

(Or: Reaching back into the recesses of your brain to help your kids with fractions, spelling, and the best places to plant plastic vomit)

Are you equipped to help your children with their homework? Are you aware of the latest trends in education? Do you know what the phrase "child-centered learning" means? Do you know the name of your child's teacher? Do you even know what grade your kid is in?

To get a sense of where you stand, answer the following True/False quiz.

1. An Integer is a car made by Acura. **T or F?**
2. If you have a dangling participle, you're more likely to notice it if there's a cool breeze. **T or F?**
3. Xylem and Phloem are the guys who do those really gross magic acts. You know, like cutting into their arms? And one of them never talks? **T or F?**
4. They call it "long division" because it takes way longer to do it that way than to use a calculator. **T or F?**
5. A Protractor is THE best brand of riding lawnmower. **T or F?**

6. Julius Caesar was the guy who played the Joker in the old *Batman* series. **T or F?**
7. They called it The War of 1812 because Canada got 18 points, and the U.S. only scored 12. **T or F?**
8. The largest Continent is the Lincoln. It also has the best trunk space. **T or F?**
9. In subtraction, you can't borrow from the next column unless you have a good credit rating. **T or F?**
10. The Pluperfect Subjunctive is the best thriller Robert Ludlum's ever written. **T or F?**

How did you do? If you answered even one of these questions as "True," you probably distinguished yourself during your school years as the student voted most likely to spend his life as a rutabaga. Or, worse, a TV sitcom writer.

But the fact that you may have answered several of these questions as "True" is no reason to think you can't be there for your kids when they run into problems with their homework. You are, after all, a parent, with many years of life experiences, and while you may not have been the BEST student in your school, you could always be counted on to have the most realistic-looking plastic vomit.

Sadly, most fathers retain little of what they learned in school, except how to make farting noises with their armpits, and the two basic ways to look as though you're spitting without actually doing it.[1]

But when your children ask for your guidance with such things as fractions and multiplication and spelling, you may be able to access, back in the deepest, most-hidden recesses of your brain, some memories of what you were taught as a kid.

---

[1] Okay, okay, here they are:
a) Gather some spittle on lip, lunge forward as if to expel, but actually inhale it suddenly.
b) Flick index finger over pursed lips as you are exhaling. Works best from behind intended victim, on hair.

175

And if not, you can fake it by always answering a question with a question, for example: "And what do YOU think the square root of nine would be?"

How Far Should You Go?

This is a very tough question for parents. You want to help your children do their very best, but at the same time, you don't want to do their whole project for them, especially if *Coach* is coming on in 10 minutes.

How much, you wonder, are the OTHER parents helping THEIR kids? What do you do, for example, when the students start studying the early years of space exploration, and the child who shows up with a life-size working model of the lunar landing module happens to be Neil Armstrong's little brat? Are you supposed to believe he did that all on his own? How the heck are you supposed to compete against that?

Well, you can't worry about it. You have to teach your kids some basic values: that the only work they'll ever feel proud of is the work they do for themselves.

Unless, of course, your child tells you at 9:30 one night, tears streaming down his face, that his project on the Trent-Severn waterway system, with a detailed, working model of the Peterborough lift locks, is due the next morning, and the only reason he forgot all about it is he's been so darned worried about all the stress YOU'VE been going through at work, and won't you please, PLEASE help or the teacher is not only going to kill him, but call YOU in for an interview and ask if it's really true, that your son is having trouble concentrating on his studies because his mother has left you for the lion tamer at the Ringling Bros. Circus.

Generally, however, the best thing to do is to give children the skills and guidance they need to complete their assignments on their own. Monitor their progress, make sure they're meeting deadlines, that they aren't leaving everything to the last minute.

Often the best way to achieve this is to lead by example:

Dad: (adopting his extremely wise tone) Now, what you have to do, precious, is get yourself organized. Decide how much time will be needed to get this assignment finished, then assess how much time you'll need each night to get it done at a reasonable pace.

Daughter: Dad, what's the date today?

Dad: It's the 28th of April, sweetheart. I hope that doesn't mean you've left it too late.

Daughter: I don't think so, Daddy. But when do you have to have your tax return in by?

Dad: Uh, well, uh, that would, gosh, I suppose that would be April 30, honey. Just, uh, two days from now.

Daughter: How's that coming along, Daddy?

Dad: (suddenly sweating) Have you seen Daddy's shoebox, sweet-cakes, the one where I save all those little pieces of paper, receipts, and that kind of thing?

Daughter: Is that the one I used to bury Chuckles the hamster after he got squished under the couch cushions?

Know What the Assignment Entails

Have a good idea what it is, exactly, the teacher is looking for.

For example, if your daughter comes home seeking suggestions about how to make a really terrific poster for "Anti-Bullying Week," it may be helpful to know what the school's motivations are in having students take on such a task.

"I have the perfect idea," you might say. "We need a strong, simple slogan for your poster, something catchy that's sure to gain you a terrific mark."

And you come up with: "Death to Bullies."

"Gee, Dad, I'm not so sure about that," your daughter says.

Nonsense, you say, helping her produce a poster so detailed, so powerful, and so graphic, that it could be used to promote the new

Arnold Schwarzenegger flick, *Terminator 3: Bullies on the Chopping Block.*

You can't wait until she gets home from school the next day to find out how it was received. She has even brought home a personal letter from the teacher, addressed to you (shown at left).

Or maybe your son says he needs help with his project, "All About Contractions."

Now, even though you are a dad, and were able to father a child, you must face the fact that you know absolutely nothing about what the miracle of birth actually entails once you've made your initial contribution, as it were. Your natural inclination may be to say to your son: "I think your mother could help you with that one."

But hold on, you think. If my own SON can tackle delicate human reproductive questions, then so can I. I'm not chickening out of this one.

> Dear Parent:
>
> We are obliged to inform you that the board of education, in conjunction with the local law enforcement authorties, have placed you under 24-hour surveillance.
>
> If you have any questions regarding this, please do not hesitate to call the principal, once you have obtained counsel, of course.
>
> Sincerely,
> The Teacher

"Contractions," you say, "are, of course, the opposite of expansions. When things expand, they get bigger, and when they contract, they get smaller. Now, the use of the word 'contractions' in this case is applied to a woman's pregnancy, and —"

"Pregnancy?"

"Yes, okay, WELL, clearly we have to take a step back for a second. You wait here, I think I have some pictures that would help you understand this better."

Anyway, after several hours, your son has the most spectacular health class report you could possibly imagine. He could be the first Grade 3 student qualified to open his own OB-GYN office. You anxiously await his arrival from school the next day.

"So," you say, "what did the teacher think of THAT?"

"He said it was pretty interesting, but he was kinda looking for something different, like when you say 'I cannot' but you shorten it to 'I can't.' Isn't that a contraction, too?"

Reducing Distractions

A child can't do a good job on her homework if she's unable to concentrate. If your kitchen is the center of activity, even after the supper dishes have been cleared away, then the dinner table is no place for a kid to try to memorize her provincial capitals.

And don't let her do her homework in front of the television, or she'll end up with a book report that says *Little Women* was a Stephen King tale about aliens who unleash a pack of shrunken, mutant females to chow down the citizenry of Castle Rock, Maine.

Set up a cozy, quiet corner in her room for studying, where she's away from friends and siblings and other potential interruptions.

Ask her to make a list of the things she'll find most useful to attack her studies. It probably will look something like this:

- desk and comfortable chair
- pens, pencils and paper, calculator
- private phone line with conferencing capabilities
- 586 computer with built-in TV monitor and built-in modem
- CD player
- fax machine
- full Internet access to allow communication with other students around the world, access to countless universities' libraries, completely untraceable essays written by anonymous scholars but guaranteed to win a minimum of B+, and the alt.sex. teenagers Frequently Asked Questions page
- personal tutor, preferably David Hasselhoff

Once she's all set up, just sit back and watch those grades soar! Not to mention the phone bill for that extra line you installed!

Should You Admit Defeat?

There are going to come times when you're simply unable to help your children with their homework, especially when they are dealing in concepts, like ethics, which MAY have been taught when your generation was growing up, but are not things you use anymore.

But no father likes to admit he doesn't know something, so steer your children to other resources that carry infinitely more information: the library, CD-ROMs, government agencies, their mother.

Actually, that last one may not be such a good idea. If they DO go to their mother, they're likely to repeat your excuses for not helping, and even though they may have worked beautifully on the kids, they aren't going to impress your spouse.

**Five excuses for not helping your child
get his homework done that will
absolutely, positively not wash**

1. "The dog ate my driver's license so I have to go down to the license bureau and get another one."
2. "Whoa, there's the Bat-Signal, looks like I've got to go to work."
3. "Won't the teacher be impressed when you're the only kindergarten kid to figure out the theory of relativity on his own?"
4. "Daddy would love to help, but if I did, the teacher would have me arrested and I'd have to go to jail."
5. "No speak English."

25

Pets

(Or: How to make it look like suicide when the goldfish dies)

To deal with your fatherly concerns regarding kids and pets, we turn things over to Dr. Woof, Pet Guy. Not only is Dr. Woof a widely recognized expert in pet care and a father of three, but none of those bogus charges of satanic goat rituals laid against him in the Atlantic provinces ever stuck.

Dear Dr. Woof: The kids are really hounding me to let them keep this little critter (picture enclosed) that followed them home from school the other day. It's cute enough, and it seems to understand basic commands, like sit and roll over and the like, but it eats like crazy and has to be taken out at regular intervals. I'm not convinced that we need this kind of disruption to our lives. — Desperate in Dundas.

Dr. Woof responds: Dear Desperate, it strikes me that what's at the root of your problem is that what followed your children home is not a dog, exactly, but an unemployed relative, namely your cousin Jed from Winnipeg. What really tipped me off was your comment about how much he eats. This is not uncommon behavior for unemployed out-of-town relatives who decide to drop in and stay indefinitely. They also tend to shed a lot, usually dirty laundry, which they allow to gather in large piles until someone offers to clean it for them. And you will have to take him out a lot, generally to places where he says he has a job interview, but he may kick up quite a fuss if you attempt to groom him for such an occasion.

You would probably be better off getting a dog, or even a cat, as they will not normally pour themselves four glasses of orange juice in the morning, leaving none for anybody else.

Dear Dr. Woof: The other night my daughter's gerbil escaped from his cage, and we are having some trouble trying to locate him. We're pretty sure he's still in the house, but what if he crawls into one of the heating ducts and dies there? Also, we are building in our basement, and are concerned he may have hidden between some studs that have already been drywalled over. What do you recommend? — Panicky in Peterborough.

Dr. Woof responds: Dear Panicky, you are definitely taking the right route using drywall for your basement renovations. Many people opt for wood paneling, which can often be too dark in rooms that already have very limited lighting. Just be sure you choose a light shade of paint for the drywall to give the new room an open, airy feel to it.

Whoa! Dr. Woof got just a little bit confused there, thinking that he was at his other job, Dr. Molding, Decorator Guy. Let's see if we can get back on track here.

Your daughter's gerbil is probably still alive; the trick now is to try to lure him out of his hiding place and back into his cage. What you need is the right kind of bait.

Try a small television and VCR. The VCR does not need to be in the cage, but the television does. Once you have all this set up, just slap in a video of the best of *Gerry Gerbil*, that tremendously popular children's show where gerbils get into all sorts of great adventures, driving toy cars and toy boats, all with the aid of just a few drops of Krazy Glue.

Gerbils love this show as much as children, and as soon as that familiar music comes on, your daughter's pet will be scuttling back into its cage to tune in.

Assuming of course, that the gerbil ISN'T dead behind the wall, in which case you might want to consider buying some of those plug-in air fresheners.

Dear Dr. Woof: Our son, who has taken to plastering the walls of his rooms with Nazi posters, has a pet tarantula named Bert. He is quite taken with this pet, and often stays up late at night talking to it. In fact, he talks to his tarantula a lot more than he talks to us. And more than once we have found Bert crawling across our bedcovers late at night, heading for our necks.

Our son's explanation is: "Gosh, Mom and Dad, I don't know how such a thing could happen. It sure is good he didn't bite you!" And then he starts to giggle.

We are, not to put too fine a point on it, scared. Do you think we should have him psychologically tested? — Terribly Frightened in Fenelon Falls.

Dr. Woof responds: Dear Terribly Frightened, you should know that there's been only limited success in counseling spiders. They do not take kindly to advice, and even when they do, they rarely act on it.

Since Bert is your son's spider, why don't you have him try talking some sense into it?

Dear Dr. Woof: I think there is something wrong with my son's goldfish. He has a small bowl in his room with two fish in it, and both of them have been staring at the ceiling for several days. It will break my son's heart if something has happened to them, as he will feel responsible, even though he has fed them diligently, sometimes as much as a cupful of food a day. — Worried in Wiarton.

Dr. Woof responds: Dear Worried, I think you may have a small problem on your hands, but do not despair, there are ways out of it.

These fish are exhibiting classic symptoms of what is known, in the ichthyological community, as death. But there is no reason for your son to feel that he's to blame. Even if he may have overfed the fish a tad, it's not his fault if the fish have no sense of self-control.

Sometimes having pets can provide some very valuable life lessons, even painful ones. That's why it's very important you help your child face the cold, hard reality of this situation. And your first step in helping your child face the truth is to write a convincing goldfish suicide note.

Something like "Can't go on since they canceled *Flipper*" should suffice, or even: "Goodbye, cruel sea!"

If this strikes you as unsatisfactory, you could simply remove the fish (disposing of them in the traditional way, by using them to enrich your municipal septic system) and stick a Post-It note to the tank that says: "Gone fishin'!"

Finally, if you are willing to engage in an innocent act of deception, you could go to the pet store and get two more fish that look exactly like the deceased and put them in the tank before your son gets home from school.

Don't make the mistake Dr. Woof did, however, and forget to remove the dead fish from the tank before adding the new ones. When a child finds two new inhabitants in his bowl, swimming alongside the guys who appear to be napping, he will come to some confusing thoughts about sex and death, and in which order they occur.

Dear Dr. Woof: Maybe you can help us settle a bet here. I say that the name of the pet pig in the old Green Acres *TV show was Arnold, but my wife says it was Efram Zimbalist Jr. There is a dinner at Red Lobster riding on this. Also, what was the name of the horse in* Mr. Ed? — *Hungry in Hamilton.*

Dr. Woof responds: Dear Hungry, you've won yourself a dinner. Your wife is thinking of the name of the dog in *The Simpsons*. As for the name of the horse in *Mr. Ed*, we can't recall.

Dear Dr. Woof: We agreed to let the kids have a dog provided they accepted the responsibilities that go with it. That includes walking him and feeding him. But now that we've all become attached to the fellow, they're getting very tardy about their duties. What should we do? — Tired in Trenton.

Dr. Woof responds: Do the only thing that makes sense with kids of the '90s: hire someone else to do their job for them.

There are plenty of dog-walking services now being offered. Whoever you hire should be someone who understands and likes animals, and doesn't mind being referred to as "the help" by the children who actually own the dog.

Even if your children can't handle the responsibility of caring for the dog, they should at least be able to sit in judgment of the person hired to do the work. Let them know what your expectations are of this employee, so that if the work is not completed satisfactorily, the children can say: "My dad's going to sue you if you don't do this right."

This also falls into the category of pets providing us valuable life lessons.

Dear Dr. Woof: When our cat Missy stretches out on the front step and falls asleep under the hot, afternoon sun, our kids find it amusing to hold a magnifying glass over her until she wakes up. They started with bugs, then frogs, and I can't help but feel they're working their way up to something really ambitious for when we go to the zoo to see the visiting Chinese pandas. We also had an unfortunate exploding-udder incident this summer during a trip to a local dairy farm. Do you think taking away their magnifying glass will traumatize them in a creative sense? — Dumb as a Holstein in Unionville.

Dr. Woof responds: Dear Dumb, I believe you can safely take away their magnifying glass, so long as you substitute it with something else that will provide the kiddoes with an outlet for their wild sense of fun.

Have you considered archery? There's a tremendous emphasis on hand-eye coordination in this sport, and kids really take to it. Unlike playing with a magnifying glass, it's not necessary for your target to be motionless.

Don't be too fast, however, to quash their original interests completely. As the ozone layer continues to thin, magnifying-glass activities are sure to grow in popularity, and may even be sanctioned some day by the Olympics committee. If its members can be talked into ballroom dancing, anything's possible.

Dear Dr. Woof: We paid a fortune for one of those little shih tzu dogs (picture enclosed) and we're just so busting with pride that we wanted to tell you about him. This is definitely a breed we would recommend to people with small children.

He's very furry, and we love him to bits. He's a dream to take care of, because he doesn't eat a thing, never asks to go for a walk, doesn't annoy the neighbors with incessant barking, never jumps up on the furniture, and never nips at the kids. He is, without question, the dream dog. — Satisfied in Sarnia.

Dr. Woof responds: Dear Satisfied, Dr. Woof is certainly thrilled that you are so happy with your new pet, but can't help but feel you may have been ripped off. For the money you paid, you should have gotten not just one of these, but a pair, since what you have, in fact, is a slipper.

But you are correct: slippers are low maintenance, and they make excellent travelers. There's no need to have them bouncing all over the inside of the car with you. Just pack them in a suitcase and stow them in the trunk.

26

Bedtime

(Or: "For the love of God, PLEASE go to sleep!")

No part of the day is surrounded in more ritual for children than bedtime.

And, for a parent, there's no undertaking more daunting, no task that looms more like an iceberg on the *Titanic* of one's evening, than getting a child into bed and keeping him there.

Parents can fall into bed and, within seconds, do an excellent impression of a senator pondering an important, upcoming vote. Kids, however, seem to take forever not only to actually FALL asleep, but to even get under the covers. And once they're there, they're always getting back out. Keeping just *one* child in his bed is like rounding up kittens in a basket, except that the kittens are not usually wearing Spiderman pajamas.

Bedtime is a time-consuming process because it presents so many choices and questions for children. They include:

"Do I have to have a bath?"

"Which pajamas should I wear?"

"Which stuffed toy should I snuggle with tonight?"

"What story are you going to read me? Why are you only going to read me one page?"

"Should I use the mint or regular toothpaste?"

"Can I have a drink?"

"Can I have a snack?"

"What should I dream about?"

"What should I put on in the morning?"

"Can I go to the bathroom one more time?"

"What if I can't get to sleep?"

"Can I have the light on?"

"Could I just stay up an extra half hour?"

"Could you just lie with me until I fall asleep?"

188

To allow yourself enough time to deal with these and other issues that may come up, it's wise to start the whole process early, like shortly after breakfast.

Convincing Your Child That It Is, in Fact, Bedtime

This is the father's standing, opening line on the subject of bedtime:

"Okay, let's get ready for bed, buster."

This is followed by the child's standard, opening rebuttal:

"_____"

In other words, there is unlikely to BE a response. The first time you tell a child it's bedtime, he either does not hear you or PRETENDS not to hear you.

Wait a few moments and try again.

"Okay, come on, it's time to get ready to hit the sack."

You can now expect something along the lines of "huh?" or "in a sec" or "but this is my FAVORITE show." (A "favorite" show at bedtime may be defined as: "Interesting Cloud Formations in Minsk" on the Weather Channel.)

Resistance may become more spirited: "Why do I have to go to bed so early? BRIAN (his cousin, against whom all standards are measured) doesn't have to go to bed this early."

"That is because," you say, "Brian is 23 and a night watchman. You are nine, and you cannot expect to be thrown out of this house to get your own job, as Brian was at his house, for at least another six months."

Send out little hints that bedtime is approaching. From the second floor window, shout to your child, who is engaged in a furious game of street hockey with his buddies, any one of the following:

"I'm running your bath!"

"I've turned down your covers!"

"I've laid out your favorite flannel Tiny Toons pajamas!"

189

"Mr. Bunny-wunny is waiting for you!"

The child will now come in. Not to have a bath, exactly, but to phone Clay Ruby or Robert Shapiro or one of those other attorneys who might be willing to take on a case of child humiliation and harassment. But the good thing is, you've actually got him in the house now, where you have a better chance of pouncing on him.

Bath Time

A bath before bedtime, even though it makes this whole scenario much longer, is the best way to go, since it provides you with the longest period of "clean child."

Assuming you bathe your child around 8:00 p.m., and she gets up around 7:30 a.m. (on school days) or even later on weekends, you are going to get almost 12 hours of unsoiled kid.

If you give your child a bath first thing in the morning, however, you will wonder, by about 8:59 a.m., when she runs outside to make mudpies and roll around in the grass and something that the dog deposited after chowing down half the lawn, why it is you bothered.

Children really enjoy bubble baths, but make sure you use the right kind. If your child is expecting a Lion King bubble bath, but spots you pouring in a capful from the Pocahontas bubble bath container, well, your life won't be worth a plug nickel unless you drain out what's in the tub so far and start again.

There's no use explaining that the two bubble baths are EXACTLY the same, or that the chances that the *real* Pocahontas (or a real *lion* for that matter) ever smelled as wonderful as this toiletry product are about as good as her having her TRUE story told in a Disney animated feature.

Although children profess to hate bath time, once they're in there, you can never get them out. Even though you hate to do this — it goes against everything you believe — sometimes the only reasonable course of action is to turn things over to a vindictive sibling, who will pull the bath curtain across and then do those high-pitched shrieking noises from the shower scene in *Psycho.*

This generally does the trick.

The Importance of Brushing Teeth

It's up to you to reinforce what the dentist tells your children every six months. They must always brush their teeth before going to bed.

There is one major drawback (aside from the fact that most children leave enough gobs of toothpaste in the sink and mashed into their towels to wipe out all the cavities in the southern hemisphere) to having your kids pay this much attention to dental hygiene late in the evening. And that is: loose teeth.

Children with loose teeth can never be persuaded to get ready for bed. They are terrified that once they fall asleep, these teeth will work free and be swallowed.

They are not the least bit worried about what a few jettisoned teeth in their digestive system is going to do to them in a physical sense. What they are concerned about is the potential for lost income.

If you swallow a tooth while sleeping, what the heck are you going to leave for the Tooth Fairy? An IOU? Swallowing a tooth is like being mugged by your own body, getting ripped off by your esophagus.

So if a child notices just before bedtime that one of her teeth is hanging by a thread, she will want to remedy the situation immediately, which means standing in front of the bathroom mirror, wiggling and wiggling and *wiggling* this tooth until it decides to dislodge itself.

She will no doubt enlist your assistance. If you're like most fathers, you'll be comforting and supportive, up until that moment when you see her bend her tooth out from her gum at right angles, at which point you will pass out and hit your head on the side of the bathtub.

191

This is not such a bad thing. At least now, ONE of you is getting some sleep.

Finding That Special Stuffed Friend

Most children like to take a stuffed doll or animal to bed with them. It's very comforting to snuggle up next to a furry dalmatian, Cookie Monster, or Raggedy Ann. Often, children will have a FAVORITE stuffed friend, a friend that they absolutely MUST have in bed with them or they will be unable to get to sleep.

Sometimes, these friends go missing. And they ALWAYS go missing at BEDTIME.

It usually goes like this.

"Good night, precious," you say, kissing your daughter on the forehead as you pull the covers up around her neck.

"Good night," she says, and then starts patting around under her covers. "Where's Muttsy?"

Muttsy is her beloved, brown, threadbare dog. When Muttsy was new she was large and furry, but several years of hugging, sleeping, and being forced to wear countless humiliating doll outfits that were much too small for her have taken their toll. Muttsy now looks like the poster puppy for the Stuffed Animal Rights Organization's plea for funds.

Your daughter pats under the covers some more, then reaches into the crack between the bed and the wall.

"Muttsy's gone!" she says in a panic.

"Now, now," you reply. "I'm sure she's around here someplace."

You look under the bed. You look behind the door. You look under the clothes piled on her chair.

There is no Muttsy.

You select a small, stuffed camel from the shelf. "Perhaps tonight you'd like to sleep with Casey the Camel? That would be fun, wouldn't it?"

"I don't want Casey. I want Muttsy."

"Well, we can look for Muttsy in the morning. But right now you need to get to sleep, so why don't you just snuggle up with Casey here —"

"I CAN'T GET TO SLEEP WITHOUT MUTTSY!"

So you enlist the aid of your spouse, and the search begins. Wasn't she watching TV downstairs with Muttsy? You search the family room, and the rec room, and under the kitchen table.

"Oh my God," says your wife. "I think she had it in the car, driving back from Wal-Mart, and the kids were goofing around in the backseat, and the windows were open . . ."

"Let's try to be calm," you say, while from upstairs you can hear, "Has anyone found my Muttsy?"

"Let's search the car first."

There's nothing in the backseat, except, of course, for seven assorted Pogs, three wads of chewed gum stuck to the upholstery, several crayon bits, nine million little scraps of cut-up construction paper, the head from a Power Rangers figure, and what appears to be a crumpled page ripped from a magazine, with the words "The Playboy Advisor" and a question about whether having sex up against a speaker can't hurt your woofers. (You will have to talk to your son later about where he got this.)

Still no Muttsy.

There seems no choice left but to call in the authorities.

Within minutes police helicopters with searchlights are scanning the road between your house and Wal-Mart. TV stations break in with live coverage.

"Will Muttsy be found?" the perky anchorperson asks. "Film at 11."

As CNN sets up a live feed on your front lawn (this is the biggest story since Jessica went down the well), you go upstairs to comfort your daughter, still under the covers.

"We're doing everything we can, honey," you say. "The people looking for Muttsy are professionals."

Your daughter says she'll TRY to get to sleep, slips her hand under her pillow to get comfortable, and says: "Hey, what's under here?"

Ailments

Despite millions of dollars in research being conducted in the area of pediatrics, there's still very little known about why virtually all childhood illnesses and discomforts do not manifest themselves until you give a kid a kiss goodnight.

For example, a child who, at 10:24 a.m., falls off her bicycle and scrapes her knee will continue to ride her bike, skateboard, Roller-blade, go swimming, hang upside down from a jungle gym until all the blood in her toes is mingling with her hair roots, beat up her brother, and play hopscotch on the driveway until the sun goes down. But once she's been tucked into bed, she'll tell you that her scraped knee is absolutely KILLING her and that there is absolutely NO WAY she can sleep with this intense, positively BLINDING pain.

"How is it," you may feel inclined to ask, "you were able to do all those OTHER things all day without this bothering you, but now, when I want you to get some sleep, SUDDENLY it starts hurting you?"

Be prepared for the most wounded expression you have ever seen. Witness the tears forming in the corner of the eyes. Get ready to feel like an unfeeling, heartless jerk as she blubbers: "You think I'm FAKING, don't you?"

The truth is, she's been so busy all day having fun, this is the first chance her body's had to think about how much pain it's in. So all you have to do now is distract her, make her think about something else, and this scraped knee business will all be forgotten.

Most dads try juggling. Keep three balls in the air until your daughter drifts off. If she REALLY looks awake, progress to four. Do this for as long as it takes.

The Drink of Water

Make your life easy. There are a number of ways to deal with the frequent requests for a drink of water.

1. Run a garden hose up to your child's bedroom.
2. Install a water cooler, complete with paper cone cups, next to your child's bed.
3. Put in an aquarium, with something for scooping.
4. Place a sleeping bag in the bathtub.
5. Persuade your local Evian distributor to set up its head-quarters on your kid's top bunk.

The Bad Dream

We are not talking about the child's worst nightmare here, we are talking about yours.

At about one in the morning, after you think everyone in the house is asleep, including you and your spouse, your child will come into your room with the intention of announcing that she can't get back to sleep because she's having a bad dream.

But because she is a thoughtful child, she will be hesitant to wake you. Instead, she will stand right next to you in the dark, clutching her blanket and teddy bear, staring at you, hoping that if she looks hard enough, you will be roused from your sleep.

You will become aware of her, at first, subconsciously, as though she is a figure in a dream. And then suddenly you will open your eyes, see this dark, shadowy apparition at your side, and gasp with such a sharp intake of breath that you inhale three lace-trimmed throw pillows, which you told your wife from the very beginning you weren't very fond of.

So, let's review. You've dealt with bedtime defiance, brought in the Emergency Task Force to find a missing stuffed dog, fainted as your daughter performed her own tooth extraction, and taken three years off your life imagining that your sleepless child was Freddy Krueger.

In another 18 hours or so, you get to start the whole process all over again.

27

The School Concert

(Or: "Excuse me, I'd love to stay, but I'm wanted in surgery!")

Few things are more eagerly anticipated by your grade schoolers than the school concert.

There can be several of these throughout the school year, though they are most commonly held in the month leading up to Christmas (known as The Christmas Concert), or in the spring (commonly referred to as The Spring Concert).

Aside from the school notice that will come home in your child's backpack, and remain there with the moldy remains of a peanut butter and jelly sandwich, 15 loose Lego pieces, a note from the teacher asking you to come in for an interview AS SOON AS POSSIBLE, and a piece of only slightly chewed gum that's being saved for later, there are two other significant clues for parents that the school concert is on the horizon.

1. Your child is constantly rehearsing for something. There is some evidence — the fact that your child is playing an instrument — that it is a musical number. The instrument is

197

the flute-like recorder, and the song is "Land of the Silver Birch," although you are not sure, since it also sounds remarkably like the theme to *Hawaii Five-O* or "Tubular Bells."

2. You are told by your daughter when she comes home from school one afternoon that she needs you to make an authentic soldier costume for her class's re-enactment of the War of 1812, but not to worry, she doesn't need it until the concert starts, which is at six.

Getting a Seat

If you have any interest in being able to actually see your child perform in the school concert, you'll have to get there early.

That's because the typical school concert is held in a gymnasium, which, unlike the Princess of Wales Theatre, does not have tiered seating. The flat surface ensures that if there are more than three rows of parents sitting ahead of you, you won't see your child's interpretation of a tree blowing in the wind.

You can't get tickets to the school concert through TicketMaster. That means there is no assigned seating, which puts a school production in the same category as the Who concert a few years ago in Cincinnati, where a number of fans were trampled to death trying to get as close to the stage as possible.

You do not want this to happen to you, because if it does, your child will cry all the way home that your selfish decision to have your windpipe crushed by the head of your street's Neighborhood Watch program took all the attention away from her, the only Grade 1 child talented enough to play Norma Desmond belting out her "With One Look" number from *Sunset Boulevard* (a REAL showstopper, especially when she paused for a major booger extraction).

Another reason it's so important to be seated close to the front is you need an unobstructed view of the stage to get the best shots possible with your camcorder. Most school concerts now resemble an O. J. Simpson press conference, with dozens of parents trying to get the best possible shot.

Professional news photographers who cover such important international events as royal weddings, visits by heads of state, and strolls by Madonna where she takes her top off, will tell you that it's important to stake out a position early and hold on to it.

Sometimes crouching in the aisle is preferable to taking a seat. To ensure a good floor spot it may be necessary to head over to the school several hours early, even if that means you're slightly in the way as the Grade 8s hold a basketball practice.

Don't be afraid to jockey for position with other parents. If someone gets in front of you, you can take the more moderate approach and give them the kind of look you normally reserve for people who check out 15 things at the 1–10 express cashier at the grocery store.

But you'll make your position clearer if you take one of your child's black magic markers and use it to color in the lens of the other parent's video camera.

Scalping

Although scalping seats at a school concert may be frowned upon by your local parent–teacher association, it's a great way to score a bit of change on the side and teach your children a valuable lesson in entrepreneurship.

If you're afraid this may embarrass your child, there's no need to do it at your child's own school. Any educational institution will do.

Get to the school early and "reserve" a few good seats at the front by hanging coats over the backs of chairs. Then hang around the hallway leading into the gym a few moments before the concert is scheduled to begin. Last-minute parental stragglers will be shocked to see the entire room filled. Get their attention with a simple "pssst!"

When they sidle over, say, "Listen, you want a couple of good seats up front, maybe I can help you out." Give them a wink and rub your thumb and fingers together to make sure they understand what you're getting at.

Once you've negotiated a price, show them to their chairs and retrieve your coats. About $10 to $20 is fair, but double that for parents who have more than one child in the concert.

If they balk, tell them: "So, you don't mind paying inflated prices to see a bunch of overpaid, spoiled-brat ballplayers, but you're not willing to go the distance for your own child? Just what kind of parent are you, anyway?"

This generally works. If they continue to act offended and threaten to inform the principal, don't sweat it. You, of course, were smart enough to have seen him and the vice-principal earlier in the day, and agreed to cut them in for an appropriate percentage.

When to Leave

Children's concerts are usually presented in grade order. In other words, the kindergarten and younger grades go first, finishing up with the oldest kids.

For example, if the school is a kindergarten–Grade 8 one, and your child is in Grade 7, you will have to sit through most of the program to see your own child. But because getting a seat is so difficult (see above) you can't really arrive late.

Things are not nearly so difficult for the parents of children in the early grades, however. Once they have finished singing "Frosty the Snowperson" (an old classic updated for '90s sensibilities) and head offstage for their classrooms, you can be out of there like a shot.

The trick is finding a way to leave gracefully. You'll find most parents are intimidated into being tremendously polite. They don't want the other parents of children in the older grades grumbling about how rude they were to walk out before the show was over. It's just this kind of old-fashioned thinking that can make for a very long evening.

The best thing is to carry a beeper or cell phone with you. Before the program begins, find out the approximate time your child's performance finishes. Add on another five minutes to be sure, and at that prearranged time have a friend, relative, or secretary call you.

Now it's ringing in the concert, and you grab it from your coat pocket as quickly as you can. Whisper into the phone or read your beeper, shake your head like you are INCREDIBLY annoyed, then get to your feet and make your way out of the gym. To at least three or four people, say quietly: "I'm so sorry, but I've been called into emergency surgery."

Of course, this goes over a lot better if you are a surgeon. If you aren't, you will have to come up with an alternative. Some of these can be tough. For example, if you are a cosmetician who does people's "colors," you may not get as much sympathy telling the other parents: "My God, I have to go, Mrs. Williker just found out she's a summer, not a fall."

Even if you're NOT a doctor, but no one knows what you do for a living, you can always try the emergency surgery line, but there can be drawbacks — particularly if on your way out you're called upon to assist someone having a heart attack, and the best medical treatment you can think of is to offer him a Chiclet.

You'll get out of the concert early, but it'll cost you a $4 million malpractice suit.

(The "emergency surgery" line may also be used at communions, weddings, and your neighbor's Disney World slide presentation.)

After the Concert

Although some kids will be happy to settle for cash, praise is the most important thing you can give them after their performance.

Tell your son that not only did he do a marvelous job on the triangle, but wasn't it super that he was able to show off the Power

Ranger underwear he got for his birthday, by way of that open zipper.

And tell your daughter her role in the choir's performance of "Can You Feel the Love Tonight?" from *The Lion King*, was magnificent, even though you weren't able to see anything but her left ponytail because that miserable Billy Middlehopper with a head the size of a pumpkin was standing in front of her.

(Make a note for next year to phone the Middlehoppers, say it's the school calling, and let them know that the concert their son is in has been moved to the following night.)

When you get home, hook up the camcorder to the TV so that the entire family can watch a virtual instant replay. Listen to your child say, at least 198 times, "I look like a geek! Oh God, I look like such a MAJOR geek! I HATE it! Rewind it so I can see it again! Oh God, I look so STUPID!"

Then carefully label the tape. Include the following information:

1. Date of performance.
2. Age of child at the time.
3. Name of teacher.
4. Length of performance, in minutes and seconds.
5. Any special settings for sound and lighting that may have been utilized during the taping.

Then put the tape on the shelf and forget about it. No one will ever look at it again.

28

Watching Television

(Or: The lost *Leave It to Beaver* Episodes, including "Eddie Haskell Gets 15 to Life")

As long as there has been television, there have been concerns about how much of it children should be allowed to watch, especially if you have only one set and there's something on YOU want to watch.

Is all television bad? Are there some shows that really are worth watching? What about all the sex that's on the tube these days? How come you're not having that kind of fun?

And what about violence? Every second month the government launches another study into the effects television violence has on children, which can actually PROMPT violent incidents as bureaucrats drop anvils on each other deciding who will get one of the lucrative commission seats.

And isn't TV pushing the limits in ways it never did before? When we were growing up, shows oozed goodness and morality. There was *The Andy Griffith Show*, *Petticoat Junction*, *The Waltons*, *Father Knows Best*. Programs that stressed honesty, integrity, family values.

Take *Leave It to Beaver*. One can only imagine the kinds of episodes you'd be seeing if this show were being made in the '90s:

1. "June's New Job": June, feeling unfulfilled in her role as a housewife, starts a part-time job as a dominatrix. The mix ups begin when Beaver, spotting his mom's new whip collection, thinks his parents have bought him a pony.

2. "True Love": Lumpy confesses his real feelings for Wally, and reveals, finally, just how he got his nickname.

3. "The Detention": Beaver learns a valuable lesson when Miss Flanders keeps him in after school for bringing a loaded .45 into the classroom, and emptying it into Gilbert, who denied the Beav a peek at his test answers.

4. "Ward's Other Life": June demonstrates what it means to be an understanding wife when she takes her husband shopping for his own half-slips and pumps.

So, What's Appropriate?

Fathers must be very careful when assessing what programs are suitable for their children.

When it comes to what they'll permit, sometimes dads are a little more tolerant than moms, or, depending on the point of view, criminally negligent. Occasionally, they will make mistakes, as the following chart indicates.

Ten excuses to tell your spouse for having allowed your seven-year old daughter, who is now terrified and in bed with you, to watch *The X-Files*

1. We can't protect our children from the real world forever; sooner or later, kids have to learn the plain, awful truths about alien abduction.

2. The *X-Files* isn't just scary, gross stuff — there's things

about Nature as well, like who would have known that a python could eat a school principal whole?

3. Isn't it good for young girls to see a woman, in this case FBI agent Dana Scully, in a strong, nonsubservient role, even if she is about to have her head chopped off by satanists?

4. I thought it was *Shining Time Station*, you know, the episode where the slithery vampire is waiting for Thomas the Tank Engine in the tunnel?

5. Don't you think the scene where all the knives were flying through the air will teach our daughter the importance of responsible cutlery use?

6. You have to admit, she looks darn cute sleeping there between us, and by the way, is that the new negligee you said you bought to surprise me with one night?

7. She said she wasn't interested in watching the movie I'd rented for her, *The Devil's Cheerleaders*.

8. Oh, and I suppose YOU'D have known that worms sprouting from someone's neck would scare a seven-year-old?

9. It was the episode where the guy squeezes through the air ducts to get to his victims, and I was too scared to watch it alone.

10. *X-Files*? That was *The X-Files*? I just thought it was the news.

After you've made a few viewing mistakes of this kind, you'll have a better idea of what is suitable. Ask yourself the following questions about a TV show your child wants to watch:

1. If the school finds out, will we be in big trouble?

2. Is there anything in this program that, if my child emulates it, will cause my house insurance rates to skyrocket?

3. Will the program introduce new words to my child's vocabulary that might be used at inopportune times? For example, at Christmas dinner with the grandparents, is there a chance my child will ask: "So, grandpa, have YOU ever been with a hooker?"

If the answer to any of these questions is Yes, consider turning off the TV, or at the very least, switching to another channel. Of course, what's on the OTHER channel will be even worse, so the best course might be something as quaint and wholesome as the radio, where your child can groove to the oldies, maybe catch a nostalgia station running an old radio play, or listen to thoughtful radio talk-show hosts explain where best to aim if you want to be SURE of dropping that federal agent dead in his tracks.

Needless to say, with all the things you have to worry about on television, the last thing you want to do is give your child a set of her own for her bedroom.

Better that she listen to her CD collection instead. You'll breathe a sigh of relief when, instead of some racy prime-time sex-obsessed soap, you hear blaring from her room the Boyz II Men discussing how they want to make love to her.

Are Cartoons Too Violent?

As we mentioned earlier, there is much concern about violence in television, and this is especially true in the case of cartoons.

What's the effect on children of watching Wile E. Coyote plunge down a canyon after being foiled in his latest attempt to catch the Road Runner? Of witnessing a 20-ton rock land on his head? Of seeing a bus emerge from the fake tunnel he's painted on a mountainside and mow him down? Once a child has picked himself up off the floor from laughing, are there lasting impressions to worry about?

You bet there are. Studies have shown that young children exposed to such animated anarchy exhibit a tendency, whenever they confront coyotes face to face, to drop immense boulders on them.

Executives of the major studios that produce these cartoons are being pressured to change their approach — to develop a cartoon that's entertaining, funny, and nonviolent at the same time.

That's why your kids will soon be watching the new cartoon series *The Road Runner: Fun with Conflict Resolution Techniques, in Technicolor!* in which the bird and the coyote put aside their differences to look for a solution to world hunger. It sounds a bit dry, admittedly, but at least there's a scene at the end where a grain shipment gets dropped on the Care Bears.

In many areas, fathers concerned about violent programming can contact their local cable companies and have a so-called "V chip" installed. This chip detects programs that are deemed too violent for children, and blacks them out.

But many cable subscribers say this does not go far enough. So more chips are on the way:

The "IA" Chip: This would block out "incredibly annoying" programming, thereby wiping out all sitcoms with wiseguy, know-it-all kids who, whenever they open their mouths, provoke enough canned laughter to fill a year's supply of Campbell's soup tins.

The "N" Chip: Installation of this item would block out the most violent, sex- and perversion-filled program of them all, the "news."

The "SNL" Chip: You'll never have to worry again about a movie starring any current or former cast members of *Saturday Night Live* appearing on your TV. Leave this one activated all the time, even when it's the adults' turn to watch the tube. (This is also available from some cable outfits as the "CC," or "Chevy Chase," chip.)

Alternatives to Television

Once you've decided it's wrong to park your kids in front of the tube for six hours a day, to allow it to become a babysitter, it will be necessary for you to become more involved with your children. You'll be expected to come up with other forms of entertainment.

You'll immediately realize what a great thing this is once you've considered the following suggestions.

Board Games

Haul out the old Scrabble board, or Life or Stratego. Tell your kids something like: "Boy, when I was a kid, we didn't have videos or a hundred channels to choose from or Nintendo games or computers. We had good old-fashioned games like these to entertain us!"

Wait till you see the excitement on their faces! (Some kids MAY give off signals that they're wondering if you grew up Amish, or that they find the prospect of sitting down with you to play Parcheesi as appealing as a major exam on decimals, but don't be fooled; they're just busy wondering how much they can sell the Sega set for because they KNOW they'll never want to play with it again.)

Gather everyone round the kitchen table as you set up the Scrabble set, explaining the rules as you put all the letter tiles in a bag.

"Okay," you say, "take a look at your letters and see if you can make a word!"

Your son goes first, making "LAME," and then, from that word, your daughter spells out "GEEKS."

You can just see how much fun this is going to turn out to be!

Twister

Spread out that plastic sheet of colored dots and get ready for a family fun extravaganza. There's nothing to bring a family closer together, literally, than having their body parts intertwined in this classic, laugh-filled game.

Chances are, however, that dads will only get one shot at playing this — not just because their kids will love it so much they'll be bringing all their friends home to join in the fun, but because after anyone over 40 puts himself into the kinds of positions Twister demands, he's generally too busy visiting chiropractors and hunting for a body brace that doesn't clash too badly with his suit.

Sing-alongs

Let's face it. Children of any age, particularly teenagers, if given a choice between (a) an evening with their friends, parked in front of the tube with a bathtub-sized container of popcorn to watch *Hockey Night in Canada*, *Seinfeld* repeats, and *Melrose Place* and (b) a chance to gather round the piano with mom and dad to sing some old standards, are going to pick the latter every single time.

Show tunes are best. *South Pacific*, *Oklahoma*, *Carousel*, and *Guys and Dolls* never fail to get the kids on board. To really make them feel a part of it, take a classic song and update it, e.g., "Can't Stop Dissin' Dat Man."

Finally, a Sacred Ritual

We've attempted throughout this book so far to offer advice that applies to sons and daughters equally. But the following involves an issue that very much concerns fathers and their sons. (Daughters also have a role to play in what we're about to discuss here, but it's a matter that a mother will want to take on, as you'll see shortly.)

There are so few sacred moments between fathers and sons these days. There is the Boy Scout dinner, perhaps, where dads can see their sons' emergence into manhood as they wrestle with fellow Scouts for the last piece of pepperoni and pineapple pizza.

In some cultures, taking your boy for his initiation into hunting is one of these moments. Or it can be sitting down with your boy to explain the mystical details of the birds and bees, although there's no reason a mother can't do this, too. In fact, she'll probably be a little surer of her facts.

With these special father–son moments seemingly in decline, it's little wonder so much significance has been attached to the kind of bonding that goes on between a dad and his boy in the most sacred of all ceremonies: the passing on of the remote control.

What cuts closer to the very heart of maleness than the TV remote?

Introducing your son to the remote is an occasion immersed in ritual. When a boy is three or four years of age, sit him down in the family room in front of the TV, surrounding yourself with bowls of cheese sticks, potato chips, and Fresca.

A few words are in order for this special moment.

"This little black box, my son, which fits so comfortably in your hand, is your gateway, your portal to the world. It is no coincidence that it looks identical to the obelisk in *2001: A Space Odyssey*. It is a force greater than any other in the universe. It is a mystery older than time.

"It lets you change channels without getting up."

The child will look at you with wonder in his eyes and drool on his chin. You continue:

"Not just change channels, but FLIP through them, at lightning speed. Let me show you *(big dramatic pause here)*, my son."

And you demonstrate, starting at Channel 2, then zooming on from there. A split second of Columbo in his raincoat, Jerry Springer and a one-legged transvestite who slept with his wife's sister, the Weather Channel (cloudy, overnight low of 16°F), Bob Barker asking the guy from Ohio in plaid golfing slacks and a different plaid shirt which costs more, the Tuna or the Hamburger Helper, the Cookie Monster —

"Hey!" says your son.

— a local cable interview with neighborhood author Beatrice Mutton discussing her new book *No More Stamens: A Feminist Gardener's Guide*, a sports network repeat of last night's NHL game, a documentary on the inexplicable absence of volcanoes in Saskatchewan.

"And there is so much more," you continue. "But the moment has come for you to explore this world for yourself. So I present to you *(cue John Williams music)* this television remote control."

And you place it ceremoniously in the hands of your son, and for just a moment, your hand, your son's, and the remote are one.

The circle is complete.

Slowly, holding your breath, you pull away your empty hand. The remote is now in your son's control. He gums it.

You're forgiven if you suddenly feel the urge to cry. In this instance, it's a very manly thing to do.

(Now that word about girls we promised. In their heart-to-heart with their mothers, girls are taught a variety of life skills, including the 10 best places to hide the batteries for the remote, how you can use the channel changer on the VCR remote to counteract the TV remote, and how to apply thick, clear tape on the TV sensor so the remote won't work regardless of how hard the doofus on the couch pushes the buttons.)

29

The Vasectomy

(Or: "DAAAAAAAADDDDD, what the heck are you doing in there? I have to go to the bathroom!")

Once their family is well underway, a husband and wife often reach a point where they must make a major decision.

We are NOT talking about the decision whether to have more children. That one, for many couples, is made much earlier. Many women make it RIGHT IN THE DELIVERY ROOM. And many men make it after their kids borrow their golf clubs to determine whether the family car's fenders are made of that new plastic material that bounces right back, and conclude that, in fact, they are not.

No, these couples are faced with a major decision about birth control. And, again, we are not talking about some simple pharmacy purchase here. We are talking about something permanent.

We are talking SURGERY.

Because Today's Man has come a long way, and because he understands that his wife has already been through enough, what with pregnancy and vomiting and childbirth and stitches and breasts so sore that if he even LOOKS at a picture of them in a snapshot taken of her on the Clearwater beach in 1987, she will scream in agony, he is more than willing to make a major sacrifice with regard to a more permanent birth control arrangement.

He is willing to actually take the day off work to drive his wife to the hospital so that she can have her tubes tied.

Many women, who fail to understand just how far men have come in developing progressive attitudes, remain unimpressed with this kind of sacrifice, and are demanding more.

They are demanding that their husbands put their hoozits under the knife.

The operation is called a vasectomy, from the Latin "vas," which means "you'd be better off," and "ectomy," which means "just giving up sex altogether."

So you book an appointment with your doctor, who explains, through the use of absolutely disgusting medical diagrams, exactly what he will do to you to render you infertile.

He will be taking a section out of two tubes, he says, called vas deferens, which is just bad spelling for "vast difference" — so named because the kind of fun you have on the operating table while they do this to you is vastly different from the kind of fun you normally associate with this area of your anatomy.

You are not to worry about this operation making you any less of a man, the doctor says. He needn't waste his breath, because you already know what kind of a man you are, seeing as how you've allowed your wife to talk you into coming in here to have this done to you.

Having the Operation

The operation is quite simple, usually done on an out-patient basis at your local hospital. You drive in, get undressed, have your operation, put your clothes back on, get back in your car, and make whimpering noises like a dog that's just been fixed as you depress the clutch pedal.

The doctor will have you lie flat on your back on the operating table. Even though lying on your stomach may seem like a good idea to you, all attempts to do this will be thwarted.

Operating cloths will be draped all over you, except for the area where the surgery is to be performed, leaving that part of you looking like a miniature mutated shrub with a big nose.

At this point, the doctor will produce an extremely large needle, about the size of a harpoon, to freeze you so that the incisions he's about to make will not hurt. There are three things you can do here to make this go a little more easily.

1. Run.
2. Clasp your heart and feign intense pain, in the hope that they will abandon the vasectomy and perform a triple bypass instead.
3. Ask for gas.

Once the operation is finished, and you get home, you may notice some tenderness in this area for a few days. If you tame bucking broncos for a living, it might be wise to ask for a couple of days off. Also, if you are an accountant. Either way, you're going to want to put your feet up and take it easy.

For the first few days, should you happen to subscribe to a cable service that runs hot, sexy movies, totally uncut, DO NOT WATCH THEM, unless you want to hear a strange tearing sound coming from your shorts.

Providing the Sample

A few weeks after you have had a vasectomy, you will be required to bring a sperm sample into the medical center's laboratory for testing, to see whether there are any of those guys, those ones who in the past have been so eager to get babies started, still swimming in there. "How am I supposed to do this?" you ask.

Don't be coy. You are now expected — NO, you are now being *compelled* — by the medical community to perform a task that through your entire adolescence, and no doubt beyond, you have performed diligently and with great skill. It has been, throughout your life, one of the few things that you are really good at, even though you are reluctant to put it on your resume.

And now you're acting like you don't know what they're talking about.

Although, to be fair, the language that is sometimes used by the people at the lab can sometimes throw you off a bit. For example:

Male: (phoning discreetly from the office) Uh, is this the lab?

Nurse: Yes it is. (Just so you know, it will ALWAYS be a woman that you deal with whenever you have any questions regarding your sperm sample. This is all part of the health care plan to discourage you from abusing the system — or yourself — too much.)

Male: I, uh, have to bring in, uh, a sample, uh, to see whether, uh, well, you know, I had an operation, and, uh, they said I, uh —

Nurse: (in a voice loud enough that it can be heard coming out of the receiver five desks away) IS THIS A SPERM SAMPLE?

Male: Uh, yes.

Nurse: Fine, just bring it in and we'll take care of it. But remember — and this is very important — collect it within an hour of bringing it to the lab.

Male: (totally baffled) You mean, after I've dropped it off, you want me to come back an hour later and take it home with me? I, uh, really don't need it back.

Nurse: (completely exasperated) I mean, you must COLLECT the sample at home, and then, within an hour, get it to the lab so that it is still fresh enough for testing. *Collect.* Do you understand what I mean by the word *collect*? Do I have to paint you a picture?

Male: NO. Of course not. I knew that was what you meant.

Now comes the real moment of truth. The actual *collecting* of THE SAMPLE that will be taken to the lab.

The only convenient time to drop this off at the lab is on your way to work, since they're closed by the time you get home. Which means that the sample must be collected in the hour BEFORE you leave for work.

Here is a partial list of things that typically must also be done in the hour before you leave for work:

- try to rouse your kids from sleeps so deep, that if they were accident victims, you'd conclude they were in irreversible comas.
- talk your daughter, once she comes down to breakfast, out of wearing the red and green plaid top with the neon purple Barney shorts.
- help your wife find her blue silk top which she swore was on the top shelf in the closet but isn't now and what happened to it and did YOU put it someplace, as if you even KNEW she had a blue silk top?
- read or fill out 14 notices your children suddenly present to you, 8 of which are for out-of-school trips (1 to China) and require checks for varying amounts to be made out to the school, and 6 urgent requests for interviews because there is some concern about your son's repeated attempts to set the school on fire.
- move your car out of the driveway so your wife will be able to get her car out, once she's found her blue silk blouse (which she has not) and is ready to go to work.
- clean up bowl of spilled corn flakes (milk already poured) that your daughter accidentally knocked to the floor while attempting to render her brother unconscious by slamming him in the head with her 10-pound binder.
- rush son to Emergency to see if there's any cranial damage.
- race back in time to catch two slices of whole wheat flying out of the toaster.
- notice odd spot on tie, rummage through closet trying to find

another one that matches the shirt and suit you are already wearing, and conclude that you only have one tie that DOESN'T have a stain on it, and it does NOT match your suit, so you will have to change everything.

Now, you must add to this list:

• get romantic with yourself.

So you find a moment and lock yourself in the bathroom. You have a specimen bottle that the lab has provided you, which is about an inch across and four inches high, with a white plastic cap.

You are suddenly overwhelmed with panic. Are you supposed to FILL THIS?

To the TOP?

But you are not going to phone the clinic again, and get that nurse. You are just going to do the best you can, and provide whatever you can to the lab.

So you get started.

BANG! BANG!

It is a knock at the door.

"What is it?" you shout.

Your eight-year-old son is on the other side. "I have to go to the bathroom, Dad. Let me in."

"Use the other bathroom."

"My *sister's* in there."

"Wait for her to come out."

"But I CAAAAAAAAAAAAANNNNNNNN'T wait. I have to go NOOWWWWWW."

"Well, you're going to HAVE to wait. Daddy's busy in here."

"What are you doing? You already shaved. I saw you shave."

"I'm going to the bathroom."

"Then how come I can hear you right by the door? The toilet isn't right by the door."

"Your sister's probably done now, go see."

Then silence. You can hardly believe it. Your son has actually done what you asked. Should you stop and phone Ripley's?

Okay, where were we now? Back to the business at hand, as it were. Now, just concentrate, think about —

BANG! BANG!

You scream at the top of your lungs, louder than you have ever screamed before: "I TOLD YOU TO GO USE THE OTHER BATHROOM!"

"It's me," says a much softer voice on the other side of the door. It is your wife. There is concern in her voice, compassion. She's every bit as troubled about this whole sample business as you are. She asks tentatively: "How's it going in there?"

You let out a breath. "Not very well."

"Maybe if I got you something to read," she suggests.

You think about this for a moment. "Okay," you say, somewhat defeated, "maybe that would speed things along a bit."

She is gone, and then there is a soft tapping at the door. "I have something for you," she says seductively.

You unlock the door and open it about half an inch, so that your wife can slide in a magazine.

"Thanks, honey," you say. "This is just all so embarrassing. Thanks for being so understanding."

And you look, and see that she has handed you *Model Railroader*.

Finally you accomplish what you have to do, imagining boxcars and tank cars and flat cars coupling and uncoupling and going into tunnels, and drop by the lab on your way to work. Waiting for you behind the counter, of course, is THAT NURSE.

"Uh, yes, uh," you say, "I have a sample that needs to be analyzed for, uh, well . . ."

"Say," says the nurse, "aren't you the guy who phoned and thought I meant you had to come back here and take your sample back home with you? Hey, Jack, Lorna!" she shouts to a back corner of the lab. "This is the guy I was telling you about! Who thought he had to come back? You know?"

And now there are three people doubled over, laughing, so much so that the nurse accidentally knocks your sample over with a file folder of printed specimen test results, and the cap has fallen off, and you don't even want to know about the rest.

So the nurse reaches into a drawer and slams a new, empty specimen container on the counter. "You'll just have to *collect* another one for us," she says, and points. "Bathroom's over there." She has what can best be described as an evil grin.

As you head over to the bathroom door, the nurse calls to you,

"Oh wait, you might need this." And tosses you a copy of this month's *Bacterial Digest*.

Anyway, a couple of days go by while you await the test results. You imagine the wild, crazy manner in which you and your mate will be able to explore the new sexual frontier, free of the encumbrances of icky, inhibiting, mood-destroying birth control devices.

Finally, the call comes in. It is the secretary at your doctor's office.

Your wiggly guys are dead. Finished. Toast. You are now packing blanks, and you couldn't be happier.

Of course, it's appropriate at this time to pause for a moment of reflection, to remember how hard these guys have worked for you in the past. Ten seconds or so should be adequate.

Just as any guy is excited to try out a new power tool after a trip to Home Hardware, your priority is to try out your new, improved equipment.

You phone your wife and tell her to skip out of the office, to meet you at home early. It is the most delicious rendezvous you've arranged since meeting at the back of the reference section in the university library.

She falls into your arms. You sweep her off her feet, carrying her into the bedroom like a new bride. And then you —

There is the sound of the front door slamming.

"HEY MOM! DAD? I'm hooooMMMME! I had a sore throat so I skipped my last class! When I saw your cars here I didn't bother going to the sitter's. What are you guys doing home so early?"

30

Dads of the Future

(Or: The Hi-Tech Wallet)

What does the future hold for fatherhood?

Will men become even more unbearably sensitive?

Will they be able to remember the names of their kids' teachers without the use of cue cards?

Will genetic advances make it possible, in the future, for men to bear children, just like in the movie *Junior*? Should we find out where research into this is being conducted, and lobby to have their grants withdrawn, and have it directed to something more useful, like figuring out why women always wave you to go ahead at four-way stops, even when they've got the right of way?

Before we can answer these and other totally irrelevant questions, and before we can get a sense of where we're headed, we must first look to the past, and at how much the father's basic role has changed since the beginning of this century.

In the early 1900s, the responsibilities of men and women were more clearly defined. The household was the woman's domain, and that

221

included most of the duties related to the upbringing of the children.

The father, however, was unconcerned with domestic matters. He was too busy blowing up mountains to make way for railroads, running dry goods stores, shoeing horses, panning for gold, or, if he held a higher station in life, walking through muddy, unpaved frontier streets wearing a top hat and tails and twirling a cane and generally passing himself off as a pompous twit.

His duties at home were limited to coming through the front door at the end of the day, whipping off that hat with great formality, handing over the cane to his wife, and asking which of the kids had left a pony in the middle of the driveway.

A father back then did not need a large repertoire of wise sayings. He could generally get by with the following:

"You watch your Ma there and you'll learn to grow up and make someone a fine wife someday."

"Keep a stiff upper lip, young man! Keep your nose to the grindstone."

"You both mind your mother, now."

"Who left oil lamps burning all over the house?"

"I'm going to need a lift tomorrow because Bessie has to go in for new horseshoes."

"I think Saturday nights are going to be a lot more interesting around here once they invent the video. But the question is, what in tarnation will we actually VIEW the movies on? And what, exactly, is a movie?"

But as this century hurtled onward, the role of fathers began to change. They took more of an interest in what was happening inside the home.

Man: (coming in the front door) Honey, I just want to say, you look terrific tonight, and after dinner I want to sit down with the kids and see how they're doing and help them with their homework and really get in TOUCH with everyone around here, throw in a load of laundry and iron my own shorts. I've been spending too much time at the office and neglecting my family far too long.

Woman: You don't live here. You live in the house next door.

Man: Oh. Sorry.

And as this interest began to grow, so did their responsibilities. This was due in large part to the increasing number of mothers who were taking jobs outside the home.

At first, most men were not thrilled with this development, and did not take on extra duties in the home without some grumbling. But over time, many found they actually liked it, particularly in areas that called upon their genetic inclination to things mechanical.

Wife: Can you finish up those dishes in the sink? The dishwasher's full.

Husband: (unable to take her word for it, and peeking inside the machine) There's TONS of room left in here, honey. Let me show you. All you have to do is rearrange things a little more efficiently, like I have in my workshop. You just have to imagine the dishes are circular saw blades and the cutlery, drill bits. Just move this over here, and this over here, and then we can take these dishes in the sink and fit one here, and we can JUST squeeze in this old antique bowl from Aunt Gwendolyn that dates back to 1876 by jamming it up against this pot for the spaghetti and . . . oh oh.

Wife: I'm leaving you.

Now we have reached the point where some fathers stay home while their wives go off to earn an income. And the way things are going with these progressive changes in attitude, in another 10 years or so, we may even have ceased referring to these alleged men as lazy, layabout wussies.

Yes, fathers are starting to do more of what have traditionally been mothers' duties. Many have taken an interest in the preparation of meals, going so far as to remember to take out some frozen ground beef to thaw in time for dinner.

They've also taken a more active role in childbirth and the care of infants.

Men are not only allowed to be with their wives in the delivery room, but EXPECTED to be there. This is more than just a chance for a husband to show his devotion to his wife and his future children. It's an opportunity to show his skills at having episodes of lightheadedness and uncontrollable retching.

Countless fathers are quite proud of their ability to change a diaper, and can often, just like that, tell you which diaper it was:

"It was in the spring of '94, along the 401 heading up to Kingston, at a Wendy's, and my 18-month-old son had just knocked a milkshake all down the front of my wife, and I said to her, since you've got to go into the ladies room ANYWAY to clean yourself off, you might as well take young Randall, who was starting to smell so high he was beginning to levitate out of his high chair, and change his diaper. And my wife gave me a funny kind of look, the kind of look that seemed to suggest that if she were behind the wheel and I was putting something in the trunk, it would take every ounce of strength she had not to put the thing in reverse and floor it. So I said what the hey I'm a dad of the '90s, why don't I change him.

"So I don't want to hear any crap about dads not pulling their weight. I think EVERY dad should change his kid's diaper, at least once."

Dads will probably become even more demonstrative in their feelings as they get more in touch with their feminine side. This is why you see more men these days willing to actually kiss their caddies after sinking a great putt.

All of this brings us to a major question.

Could it be that this latest generation of fathers, who have lived through a time where gender responsibilities have been in such a state of flux, have actually taken on too much?

Are they taking on an unfair share of the load? Can it be that women are finally having it just a bit too easy as —

(The author, now in the process of being severely whomped about the head and shoulders by a rolled-up *Vogue* in the hands of his spouse, who just happened to be looking over his shoulder while he was composing the preceding paragraph, would like to take a few minutes to collect his thoughts, reassess his position, and seek medical attention.)

As we were saying, fathers can NEVER do too much. It's only right that they start picking up the slack.

Virtual Reality Dads

Nintendo and Sega and other computer game conglomerates are rushing to see who will be the first to come out with the first "Virtual Reality Dad" program, which will allow youngsters to don special headgear and experience parenting by the father of their choice.

Players of all ages can pick a well-known personality to be their father, make a composite from several of these people, or make a dad from scratch.

Early prototypes have shown that kids are drawn to big-name movie and sports stars. Wayne Gretzky, Doug Gilmour, Charles Barkley, and Joe Carter are leading sports favorites, and entertainment figures heading the list include Arnold Schwarzenegger, Sylvester Stallone, Fred Flintstone, and Barney.

Your dad won't let you stay out until midnight? Just talk it over with the purple dinosaur.

"Hey, Barney, YOU'LL understand me."

"Hiya! Guhuu, guhuu!"

"All I wanna do is hang out with the other kids in my Grade 2 class outside McCloskey's Bar and Grill collecting beer bottle caps for our collection! Can I go?"

"I love you. Do you love me?"

"Sure, Barney!"

"Okey dokey, then!"

If kids have the super-duper Virtual Dad program, they'll be able to head off to McCloskey's without leaving their own bedroom! But if their parents have tried to save a measly $627 by not buying the slightly more expensive $1,987.98 356-bit VR-Dad Extender, they'll be faced with their children coming straight to them to let them know that they've been overruled.

Child: Hey, Pop, I just spoke to Virtual Reality Dad, which just happens to be my own creation of Pee Wee Herman and Mel Gibson, and he said he doesn't care that I haven't cleaned my room or done my homework or taken out the trash like I was supposed to, I can still go with my friends to see *Dumb and Dumber Part 2: Dumber and Dumberer.*

Dad: Why not have Virtual Reality Dad DRIVE you there?

Child: It shouldn't take me long to get those few things out of the way.

Evolutionary Changes

Is it within the realm of possibility that men will one day be able to bear children?

There is a lot of research going on in this area, and for SOME reason, the bulk of it is being conducted by women.

In a recent interview, Dr. Winona Snidefeather, director of the Male Pregnancy Project at the Men Are Pond Scum Institute, said: "We are doing all we can to see that men are able to share in the joy, the wonder, and the sheer, unbearable pain of bringing a new life into the world. You cannot IMAGINE how hard we are working on this, and we have the support of millions of women everywhere.

"We're also desperately looking for ways for men to have cramps, get sore breasts, and retain water, but it doesn't have anything to do with the male-pregnancy project, it's just for the hell of it."

Also being looked at are hybrids.

Just as there are hybrid corns and hybrid chickens, and in the pet world, breeds like the cockapoo (a cross between a poodle and a rooster) — scientists are looking at what they could combine with your basic dad gene to come up with something that would be really nifty and increase their chances of winning a Nobel Prize.

What they've come up with so far sounds like a sure winner.

It may soon be possible to genetically meld a father with an electronic banking machine.

This way, whenever a child wanted to get some cash from her father, instead of having to explain herself and endure an interrogation about what she was planning to use the money for (like it was any of HIS concern!), or being forced to listen to some song and dance about how hard he worked to get this money, she'd simply punch a few buttons on his chest until he withdrew his wallet and extracted the desired amount of moolah.

Regardless of what happens with these particular research projects, it seems inevitable that, collectively, we fathers are going to evolve into some higher kind of life form.

Ask any mothers or any kids and they will tell you.

There really isn't any other way for us to go.